Rob Nagel, Editor

THOMSON
GALE

Detroit • New York • San Diego • San Francisco • Cleveland • New Haven, Conn. • Waterville, Maine • London • Munich

THOMSON

✦

GALE

™

U•X•L American Decades, 1980–1989

Rob Nagel, Editor

Project Editors
Diane Sawinski, Julie L. Carnagie, and
Christine Slovey

Editorial
Elizabeth Anderson

Permissions
Shalice Shah-Caldwell

Imaging and Multimedia
Dean Dauphinais

Product Design
Pamela A.E. Galbreath

Composition
Evi Seoud

Manufacturing
Rita Wimberley

For permission to use material from this product, submit your request via Web at http://www.gale-edit.com/permissions, or you may download our Permissions Request form and submit your request by fax or mail to:

Permissions Department
The Gale Group, Inc.
27500 Drake Rd.
Farmington Hills, MI 48331-3535
Permissions Hotline:
248-699-8006 or 800-877-4253, ext. 8006
Fax: 248-699-8074 or 800-762-4058

Cover photograph reproduced courtesy of the Ronald Reagan Library.

While every effort has been made to ensure the reliability of the information presented in this publication, The Gale Group, Inc. does not guarantee the accuracy of the data contained herein. The Gale Group, Inc. accepts no payment for listing; and inclusion in the publication of any organization, agency, institution, publication, service, or individual does not imply endorsement of the editors or publisher. Errors brought to the attention of the publisher and verified to the satisfaction of the publisher will be corrected in future editions.

Vol. 1: 0-7876-6455-3
Vol. 2: 0-7876-6456-1
Vol. 3: 0-7876-6457-X
Vol. 4: 0-7876-6458-8
Vol. 5: 0-7876-6459-6
Vol. 6: 0-7876-6460-X
Vol. 7: 0-7876-6461-8
Vol. 8: 0-7876-6462-6
Vol. 9: 0-7876-6463-4
Vol. 10: 0-7876-6464-2

LIBRARY OF CONGRESS CATALOGING-IN-PUBLICATION DATA

U•X•L American decades
  p. cm.
Includes bibliographical references and index.
  Contents: v. 1. 1900-1910—v. 2. 1910-1919—v. 3.1920-1929—v. 4. 1930-1939—v. 5. 1940-1949—v. 6. 1950-1959—v. 7. 1960-1969—v. 8. 1970-1979—v. 9.1980-1989—v. 10. 1990-1999.
  Summary: A ten-volume overview of the twentieth century which explores such topics as the arts, economy, education, government, politics, fashions, health, science, technology, and sports which characterize each decade.
  ISBN 0-7876-6454-5 (set: hardcover: alk. paper)
  1. United States—Civilization—20th century—Juvenile literature. 2. United States—History—20th century—Juvenile literature. [1. United States—Civilization—20th century. 2. United States—History—20th century.] I. UXL (Firm) II. Title: UXL American decades. III. Title: American decades.
E169.1.U88 2003
973.91—dc21
2002010176

Printed in the United States of America
10 9 8 7 6 5 4 3

Contents

Reader's Guide

U•X•L American Decades provides a broad overview of the major events and people that helped to shape American society throughout the twentieth century. Each volume in this ten-volume set chronicles a single decade and begins with an introduction to that decade and a timeline of major events in twentieth-century America. Following are eight chapters devoted to these categories of American endeavor:

- Arts and Entertainment
- Business and the Economy
- Education
- Government, Politics, and Law
- Lifestyles and Social Trends
- Medicine and Health
- Science and Technology
- Sports

These chapters are then divided into five sections:

Chronology: A timeline of significant events within the chapter's particular field.

Overview: A summary of the events and people detailed in that chapter.

Headline Makers: Short biographical accounts of key people and their achievements during the decade.

❖ **Topics in the News:** A series of short topical essays describing events and people within the chapter's theme.

✛ **For More Information:** A section that lists books and Web sites directing the student to further information about the events and people covered in the chapter.

OTHER FEATURES

Each volume of *U•X•L American Decades* contains more than eighty black-and-white photographs and illustrations that bring the events and people discussed to life and sidebar boxes that expand on items of high interest to readers. Concluding each volume is a general bibliography of books and Web sites that explore the particular decade in general and a thorough subject index that allows readers to easily locate the events, people, and places discussed throughout that volume of *U•X•L American Decades*.

COMMENTS AND SUGGESTIONS

We welcome your comments on *U•X•L American Decades* and suggestions for other history topics to consider. Please write: Editors, *U•X•L American Decades,* U•X•L, 27500 Drake Rd., Farmington Hills, MI 48331-3535; call toll-free: 1-800-877-4253; fax: 248-699-8097; or send e-mail via http://www.galegroup.com.

Chronology of the 1980s

1980: President Jimmy Carter cancels a Washington exhibit of works from the Hermitage Museum in Leningrad to protest the Soviet Union's invasion of Afghanistan.

1980: The World Health organization formally announces the world-wide elimination of smallpox under the leadership of the Centers for Disease Control (CDC).

1980: **January 1** Physicist Luis Alvarez proposes that the extinction of the dinosaurs occurred because of a collision of an asteroid with Earth.

1980: **March** The banking industry is deregulated.

1980: **April 12** At the urging of President Carter, the U.S. Olympic Committee votes to boycott the 1980 Summer Olympics in Moscow to protest the Soviet invasion of Afghanistan.

1980: **April 13** *Grease,* the longest-running show on Broadway to date, closes after 3,388 performances.

1980: **May 18** In the state of Washinton, Mount St. Helens erupts, spewing forth 51 million cubic yards of volcanic ash, dirt, and rocks, leveling nearby forests and killing 62 people.

1980: **June 1** Atlanta entrepreneur Ted Turner debuts the twenty-four-hour news channel Cable Network News (CNN).

1981: The portable Sony Walkman becomes a huge seller, popularizing "mobile" music.

1981: The administration of President Ronald Reagan tries to down-grade sharply the nutritional requirements of school-lunch programs, including defining ketchup and pickle relish as vegetables.

1981: **January** A U.S. Circuit Court of Appeals rules that the First Amendment to the U.S. Constitution "does not require or even allow" public school officials to permit student prayer meetings in classrooms before school.

1981: **January 13** A three-month study links toxic shock syndrome to the use of high-absorbency tampons and confirms that teenagers have the highest risk of developing the malady.

1981: **March** President Reagan directs the Central Intelligence Agency (CIA) to assist contra (counterrevolutionary) forces opposed to the Marxist Sandinista government in Nicaragua.

1981: **March 30** John W. Hinckley Jr. shoots Reagan in the chest as the president walks to his limousine after delivering a speech at the Washington Hilton Hotel. Press Secretary James Brady, a Secret Service agent, and a Washington, D.C., police officer also are wounded. All recover, but Brady suffers permanent brain damage.

1981: **April 12** NASA's first reusable spacecraft, the space shuttle *Columbia,* is successfully launched from Cape Canaveral, Florida.

1981: **June** A new disease that will come to be known as AIDS is first detected among homosexual men and intravenous drug users.

1981: **July 7** President Reagan nominates Sandra Day O'Connor to be the first woman justice on the U.S. Supreme Court.

1981: **August 1** MTV (Music Television) begins broadcasting. Its first video is the Buggles's *Video Killed the Radio Star.*

1981: **August 3** Rejecting the terms of a government contract, members of the Professional Air Traffic Controllers Organization go on strike. Two days later, President Reagan fires more than eleven thousand air traffic controllers.

1981: **August 12** IBM introduces its first personal computer, with an operating system by Microsoft.

1982: Michael Jackson releases *Thriller,* which becomes the top-selling album in history.

1982: Rubik's Cube, a puzzle for which the solution proves frustrating and even obsessive for many, sells wildly in the United States and in other countries.

1982:   The U.S. Congress deregulates the savings and loan industry.

1982:   **June 30** The Equal Right Amendment (ERA) misses the deadline for ratification after it fails to get the support of the necessary thirty-eight states.

1982:   **August 10** A federal judge throws out a Louisiana creationism suit saying it had no place in federal courts; the Louisiana law required balanced treatment between the teaching of creation science and evolution science in the classroom.

1982:   **September 29** The first of seven people die in Chicago after taking Extra-Strength Tylenol painkilling capsules tainted with cyanide.

1982:   **November 13** In Washington, D.C., 150,000 observers witness the dedication of the Vietnam Veterans Memorial.

1982:   **December 2** Physicians at the University of Utah Medical Center in Salt Lake City successfully implant a permanent artificial heart in a sixty-one-year-old patient.

1983:   **March 23** President Reagan proposes the development of a defense shield, at least partly based in space, to intercept incoming missiles. Formally called the Strategic Defense Initiative (SDI), the proposal becomes popularly known as "Star Wars."

1983:   **April** The American public learns that the CIA assisted a contra attack on Nicaragua oil terminals.

1983:   **May 24** AIDS is called the nation's "number one priority" of the U.S. Public Health Service.

1983:   **May 25** The movie *Return of the Jedi* sets an opening-day box-office record of $6.2 million.

1983:   **September 29** After 3,389 performances, *A Chorus Line* becomes the longest-running show in the history of Broadway.

1983:   **November** Drexel Burnham Lambert executive Michael Milken develops the idea of using high-yield "junk" bonds. Many savings and loan institutions begin buying these types of bonds.

1983:   **November 16** Cal Ripken Jr. becomes the first player in baseball history to win Rookie of the Year and Most Valuable Player awards in consecutive seasons.

1984:   The Hewlett-Packard Company introduces the laptop computer.

1984:   The computer operating system MS-DOS, developed by the Microsoft Corporation for IBM, is used in two million computers and in more than 90 percent of IBM personal computers and compatible equipment.

1984: Run-D.M.C.'s self-titled debut album becomes the first rap album to be certified gold.

1984: January 24 Apple Computer unveils its long-awaited personal computer, the Macintosh.

1984: April 21 The CDC confirms news reports that French researchers have identified a virus thought to be the cause of AIDS.

1984: May 7 Texas repeals its textbook restriction, passed in 1974, requiring evolution to be presented as "only one of several explanations" of how the universe began.

1984: July 23 Vanessa Williams becomes the first Miss America to resign in the history of the pageant when a men's magazine announces it will publish nude photographs of her.

1984: December 11 Astronomers at the University of Arizona at Tucson announce they have discovered the first planet outside the solar system.

1985: English scientists report the existence of a giant "hole" in the ozone layer over Antarctica.

1985: Crack, crystallized cocaine that can be smoked to produce a short but intense high, is introduced into the United States.

1985: A record forty-three thousand farms go bankrupt as land prices fall and interest rates soar.

1985: The all-star recording "We Are the World," released under the name USA for Africa, becomes the hottest-selling single of the decade and raises $50 million for African famine relief.

1985: April 23 Coca-Cola announces that it is replacing its ninety-nine-year-old formula with a sweeter-tasting formula. Protests quickly convince the company to reintroduce the old formula under the name Coca-Cola Classic just a few months later.

1985: May 16 Michael Jordan of the Chicago Bulls is named the NBA Rookie of the Year.

1985: August President Reagan agrees to ship antitank missiles to Iran with the hope of winning the release of American hostages. After the missiles are delivered, only one hostage is released.

1985: **September 1** Oceanographer and explorer Robert D. Ballard, leading a joint French-U.S. team, discovers the wreck of the *Titanic* in the Atlantic Ocean 500 miles south of Newfoundland.

1985: **September 9** New York City school districts are struck by a boycott when a seven-year-old AIDS victim is given permission to attend school.

1986: Microsoft Corporation, led by Bill Gates's ingenuity in software programming and development, goes public.

1986: **January 28** The space shuttle *Challenger* explodes following liftoff at Cape Canaveral, Florida. All crew members are killed.

1986: **February 26** Robert Penn Warren is named the first poet laureate of the United States.

1986: **May** An international commission names the AIDS-causing virus the human inmmunodeficiency virus or HIV.

1986: **May 25** More than five million people form a human chain from New York City to Long Beach, California, in Hands Across America, a project organized to call attention to poverty, hunger, and homelessness in the country.

1986: **July 23** Greg LeMond wins professional cycling's prestigious Tour de France, the first American to do so.

1986: **August 28** Nobel laureates speak out at a news conference against creationism, claiming that to "teach that the statements of Genesis [in the Bible] are scientific truths is to deny all the evidence."

1986: **September 19** The federal government announces that an experimental drug, azidothymidine (AZT), prolonged the lives of some AIDS victims.

1986: **November 13** President Reagan says the United States has sent Iran a few defensive weapons and spare parts, but he denies any attempt to exchange weapons for hostages.

1986: **November 14** Wall Street businessman Ivan Boesky plea bargains with government officials, admitting he had bought stock after receiving tips about forthcoming merger bids. The day becomes known as "Boesky Day" among inside traders.

1986: **November 23** U.S. Attorney General Edwin Meese III announces he has discovered that proceeds from the sale of arms to Iran have been diverted to the contras.

1986: **December 23** Pilots Richard Rutan and Jeana Yeager complete the first nonstop flight around the globe on a single load of fuel in the experimental airplane *Voyager.*

1987: George Michael's song "I Want Your Sex" is banned from many radio-station playlists because its lyrics are considered too suggestive to be heard by young listeners.

1987: **March 9** Scientists testifying before the U.S. Congress announce that the ozone layer has undergone a sharp depletion in the last ten years.

1987: **March 19** Praise the Lord (PTL) founder Jim Bakker resigns after revelations that he committed adultery and stole funds from his ministry.

1987: **May 5–August 3** The U.S. Congress holds public hearings on the Iran-Contra scandal.

1987: **May 31** President Reagan refuses entry into the United States immigrants and aliens with AIDS.

1987: **August 10** In one of the largest leveraged buyouts in the decade, the TLC Group acquires Beatrice International Foods for $985 million, making TLC the largest black-owned firm in America.

1987: **August 16** The Harmonic Convergence, a two-day gathering of New Agers, begins.

1987: **October 11** The AIDS quilt is unfurled for the first time on the Mall in Washington, D.C.

1987: **October 23** The U.S. Senate rejects the nomination of Robert Bork to the U.S. Supreme Court.

1987: **December 6** San Francisco 49ers quarterback Joe Montana completes an NFL record twenty-two straight passes against the Green Bay Packers.

1988: As saving and loan institutions overextend their credits, experts estimate that $200 billion is needed to bail them out.

1988: Whitney Houston becomes the first recording artist in *Billboard* history to have four number-one songs from a single album; only one month later, Michael Jackson breaks this record with five number-one singles from his *Bad* album.

1988: **February 21** Before six thousand of his followers, televangelist Jimmy Swaggart tearfully confesses to an unspecified sin. Later, his ministry is taken away when it is revealed that he had sexual relations with a prostitute.

1988: **March 16** A federal grand jury in Washington, D.C., indicts John Poindexter, Oliver North, and two others on charges relating to their involvement in the Iran-Contra scandal.

1988: **May 27** The U.S. Senate ratifies the Intermediate Nuclear Forces (INF) Treaty, under which the United States and the Soviet Union agree to eliminate intermediate-range weapons from their nuclear arsenals.

1988: **June 1** The National Academy of Sciences criticizes the absence of strong federal leadership and support in the fight against AIDS.

1988: **June 27** Michigan becomes the first state to outlaw surrogate-mother contracts.

1988: **September 29** With the successful launch of the space shuttle *Discovery,* NASA resumes shuttle flights, suspended for thirty-two months following the destruction of the shuttle *Challenger* in 1986.

1989: A self-portrait by painter Pablo Picasso sells for $47.85 million, a record sum for a twentieth-century work; later in the year, that record is broken by the sale of Picasso's *Pierrette's Wedding* for $51.3 million.

1989: **March 8** The U.S. Department of Health and Human Services says it will support programs to supply hypodermic needles to drug addicts to help halt the spread of AIDS.

1989: **March 24** In the worst oil spill in American history, the oil tanker *Exxon Valdez* runs aground in Alaska, spilling almost 11 million gallons of crude oil into Prince William Sound.

1989: **May 4** Oliver North is found guilty on three felony charges: obstructing a congressional inquiry, destroying documents, and accepting an illegal gift.

1989: **June 10** The Moral Majority is officially disbanded.

1989: **August 24** Cincinnati Reds manager Pete Rose agrees to a lifetime suspension from baseball for gambling.

1989: **November 19** Scientists at the California Institute of Technology announce they have discovered the oldest and most distant object yet known, a quasar at the edge of the observable universe.

1989: **December 20** U.S. troops invade Panama and overthrow the government of Manuel Noriega, who surrenders on January 3, 1990, and is extradited to the United States, where he is tried and found guilty on drug-trafficking charges in 1992.

The 1980s: An Overview

The 1980s was unlike any other single decade in American history. Indeed, much in the decade seemed borrowed from decades before. The dominant political figure of the era, President Ronald Reagan (1911–), expressed an economic philosophy derived from the 1920s, a populist outlook borrowed from the 1930s, a can-do optimism from the 1940s, and an anticommunist stance straight out of the 1950s. Little during the decade was original or new. Everything from politics to art seemed to require some sort of precedent in order to be understood.

Reagan took office in 1981 through his ability to represent almost all things to almost all his supporters. They saw in him what they wanted and glossed over the rest. Devout Christians loved him for his pious speeches despite the fact that his opponent in the 1980 election, President Jimmy Carter (1924–), was a more diligent, practicing Christian. Millions saw Reagan as the champion of family values, although he was the first divorced president in American history. Many were fond of his populist, common-man image, while his closest associates were millionaires. Reagan was cherished as a strong leader who took a tough approach to foreign affairs, even as the Iran-Contra scandal raised serious questions about his competence as president. None of it mattered. As a figure, as a symbol of the office of the presidency, Reagan gave the nation what it wanted after the defeat in the Vietnam War, the disgrace of Watergate, and the disintegration of the economy in the 1970s.

Reagan and his wife Nancy ushered in a decade that reveled in the glitzy and the glamorous. Television programs such as *Dallas, Dynasty,* and *Lifestyles of the Rich and Famous* fed the nation's hunger for diamonds and success. Nancy Reagan's twenty-five-thousand-dollar 1981 inaugural gown set the tone for expensive style during a decade preoccupied with such wealthy figures as Donald Trump, Malcolm Forbes, and Tammy Faye Bakker. Pop singers such as Madonna and Michael Jackson became famous by striking poses and changing their appearances. Fashion models became international celebrities. Even the gritty television detectives on *Miami Vice* wore Armani suits.

It was a decade of surface and design rather than substance and content, and hype was everything. "Hype" was a slang term for a massive advertising campaign, usually implying the goods to be sold were not what the advertisers promised. Hype was prevalent in almost every level of American life in the decade, and advertising and marketing assumed new levels of sophistication. Children's television shows coordinated their activities with toy manufacturers. Soft-drink companies prominently placed their products in mainstream films. And MTV, the world's first nonstop commercial cable channel, presented twenty-four hours of music videos that acted as sensational advertisements for records and compact discs.

Hype made rock superstars out of mediocre artists, who used vocal overdubs and new music technology to gloss over their lack of talent. Sports became a multibillion-dollar business, and baseball and football players quarreled endlessly over contracts. Sporting-goods endorsements by athletes such as basketball star Michael Jordan filled the airwaves. Even artists such as Julian Schnabel had savvy agents to advance their fortunes.

Yet, with all the fortune and the hype, many in America suffered economically. As the decade began, with high unemployment and growing trade and budget deficits, the American economy seemed inefficient and overburdened. The solution proposed by Reagan and his advisors combined tax cuts and assertive leadership to spark capital investment. But it did not work exactly as planned. Instead, it advanced a growing divide between the economic classes, a transfer of wealth from the middle class to the wealthy unprecedented in American history. For the rich, the 1980s were boom times. Because of Reagan's 1981 restructuring of the tax code, the rich had more disposable wealth and they spent it in extravagant ways on art works, foreign automobiles, and hand-tailored suits. Statistically, these rich represented less than 1 percent of all wage earners in the United States.

As the 1980s closed, economic and social reality had set in: the stock market had crashed, the federal debt had soared, paychecks had gotten smaller, school test scores had dropped, the space shuttle *Challenger* had exploded, AIDS deaths had multiplied, and U.S. taxpayers had been stuck with bailing out millionaires who had gambled everything on questionable savings-and-loan transactions. Divided between rich and poor, powerful and weak, the United States seemed less and less a world power.

chapter one *Arts and Entertainment*

Chronology

. . . .

1980: President Jimmy Carter cancels a Washington exhibit of works from the Hermitage Museum in Leningrad to protest the Soviet Union's invasion of Afghanistan.

1980: April 13 *Grease,* the longest-running show on Broadway to date, closes after 3,388 performances.

1981: The portable Sony Walkman becomes a huge seller, popularizing "mobile" music.

1981: The University of Pennsylvania Press publishes the complete, unedited version of Theodore Dreiser's novel *Sister Carrie,* first published in 1900, including thirty-six thousand words that the original publisher, Frank Doubleday, considered too sexually explicit.

1981: August 1 MTV (Music Television) begins broadcasting. Its first video is the Buggles' *Video Killed the Radio Star.*

1982: Michael Jackson releases *Thriller,* which becomes the top-selling album in history.

1982: Compact discs (CDs) are introduced by the Sony Corporation of Japan and Philips of the Netherlands.

1982: Steven Spielberg's movie *E.T.: The Extra-Terrestrial* earns a record $235 million at the box office in only three months.

1983: May 25 The movie *Return of the Jedi* sets an opening-day box-office record of $6.2 million.

1983: September 29 After 3,389 performances, *A Chorus Line* becomes the longest-running show in the history of Broadway.

1984: Run-D.M.C.'s self-titled debut album becomes the first rap album to be certified gold.

1984: February 25 Michael Jackson wins eight Grammy Awards for his album *Thriller,* which tops thirty-seven million copies in sales and also earns him seven American Music Awards.

1984: June 19 The Motion Picture Association of America institutes the PG-13 rating.

1985: Madonna's *Like a Virgin* becomes the first album by a female artist to sell more than five million copies.

1985: The all-star recording "We Are the World," released under the name

USA for Africa, becomes the hottest-selling single of the decade and raises more than $50 million for African famine relief.

1985: **July 13** The Live Aid concert held in London and Philadelphia is broadcast to more than 1.6 billion people around the world and raises $70 million for African famine relief.

1985: **September 22** Farm Aid, a concert organized by Willie Nelson, Neil Young, and John (Cougar) Mellencamp to raise funds for American farmers, is held in Champaign, Illinois.

1986: **February 26** Robert Penn Warren is named the first poet laureate of the United States.

1986: **May 5** Cleveland, Ohio, is chosen as the site for the Rock and Roll Hall of Fame.

1987: George Michael's song "I Want Your Sex" is banned from many radio-station playlists because its lyrics are considered too suggestive to be heard by young listeners.

1987: **October 5** Thirteen New York dance companies perform a *Dancing for Life* benefit for AIDS research.

1988: Whitney Houston becomes the first recording artist in *Billboard* history to have four number-one songs from a single album; only one month later, Michael Jackson breaks this record with five number-one singles from his *Bad* album.

1988: Total spending for cultural events, $3.4 billion, exceeds spending on spectator sports for the first time in American history.

1988: **September 2** Bruce Springsteen, Sting, Peter Gabriel, and Tracy Chapman launch a benefit concert tour for Amnesty International, a worldwide organization dedicated to freeing political prisoners.

1989: A self-portrait by painter Pablo Picasso sells for $47.85 million, a record sum for a twentieth-century work; later in the year, that record is broken by the sale of Picasso's *Pierrette's Wedding* for $51.3 million.

1989: Willem de Kooning's *Interchange* sells for $20.7 million, a record for a living artist.

1989: Motion pictures gross a record $5 billion.

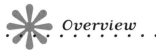

Overview

The 1980s was a decade preoccupied with success and image, and much of American art during that decade was shaped by this preoccupation. In a time of excess, art became bigger. Painting, theatrical musicals, and pop recordings all became bigger in scope and ambition, bigger in theme, bigger in budget, and bigger in promotion. The new scale and influence of art suited Americans in the 1980s. With more disposable income than in the 1970s and weary of the pessimism of that decade, they wanted to enjoy themselves again. Aided by the healthiest national economy since the 1960s, Americans began to spend more money on arts and entertainment. Prices in the art market reached new heights as the wealthy discovered that acquiring fine art was a way to demonstrate their financial success. More than ever, they came to look upon art as a business. The financial bottom line became the ultimate purpose of an art form.

Artists quickly picked up on the increased public demand for their work. Often, they marketed their work in such a way as to create and extend that demand. Pop artist Keith Haring, who drew inspiration from graffiti on city buildings and subways, created a line of products bearing his most popular graphic images. He then opened a store to sell them. Other artists were so skillful at marketing their work that the work itself became secondary. They became advertisements for themselves. Perhaps the most skilled at the sale of image was Madonna. As she marketed her movies, videos, recordings, and ever-changing image, she became a one-woman business, making millions of dollars in the process.

The most successful artists and performers of the decade learned to use the media to package and market their public images and to create a demand for their projects and products. As the public demanded more, the media gave them more. In the early 1980s, MTV hit the airwaves with a constant, twenty-four-hour-per-day stream of music videos. Continuing the decade-long madness for image, musicians and groups were soon measured by their looks as well as by their sound. A new generation of video pop stars arose, catapulted to stardom from a merging of film and music. Thanks to exposure in videos and movies, break dancing, rap music, and other forms of hip-hop culture soon spread from urban ghettos to suburbia. Pop culture became a melting pot of fashion, image, hipness, trendiness, and attitude.

The 1980s was not a decade of greed, style, and self-promotion for everyone. Some artists and entertainers became involved in social causes. Others used their work to make political statements. English musician Bob Geldof organized the Band Aid project in 1984 and the twin Live Aid concerts in London and Philadelphia in 1985 to aid victims of famine in Africa. His work inspired the USA for Africa collaboration that produced the 1985 all-star pop anthem "We Are the World." The Farm Aid concert held that same year sought to raise money to pay off the debts of American farmers. Other benefits helped raise public awareness of the discriminatory practices of the South African government and of the AIDS epidemic, which received little serious attention by the U.S. government during much of the decade.

While Americans spent lavishly on art during the 1980s, the American government under President Ronald Reagan tried to cut federal funding of the arts. His fellow conservative politicians disapproved of government agency support for artists whose works the politicians considered to be morally offensive. This culture war, with various groups trying to impose their definitions of art on everyone else, extended across America. Conservative and Christian groups throughout the nation fought to censor or ban art they considered indecent, history books they considered biased, rap music they considered violent, and movies and videos they considered irreverent. In some communities, school boards tried to remove "controversial" books from school libraries, many of which were classic novels written by respected American writers.

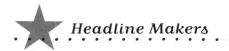

Keith Haring (1958–1990) Artist Keith Haring loved the raw energy and sense of life in subway graffiti. Drawing inspiration from it for his own work, he created images that often resembled thickly outlined hieroglyphics or cave drawings. His work became perhaps the most universal, influential, and popular art of the 1980s. In addition to creating paintings that were displayed in museums, Haring also created murals for schoolyards and on the sides of inner-city buildings. In 1986, three Haring works were placed in the sculpture garden at the United Nations headquarters in New York City. **Photo reproduced by permission of the Keith Haring Foundation.**

Whitney Houston (1963–) Singer Whitney Houston released her self-titled debut album in early 1985 to critical and commercial acclaim. Filled with conventional pop ballads and dance numbers, the album stayed at the top of the music charts for forty-six weeks and sold over thirteen million copies. Houston's powerful vocal talent was further featured on her next album, *Whitney,* released in 1987. It was the first album by a female singer to debut on the top of the *Billboard* charts. Between 1985 and 1988, Houston had seven consecutive number-one hit songs. **Photo reproduced by permission of Arista Records, Inc.**

Stephen King (1947–) Stephen King was possibly the most prolific and most famous novelist of the 1980s. A one-man best-seller factory, he turned out as many as four novels in a single fifteen-month period. By 1985, there were fifty million copies of King's horror books in print, earning him more than twenty million dollars. He earned three million dollars alone as an advance for *It* (1986), which was ranked number one on the *New York Times* best-seller list before it was officially published. Many of his bestsellers were quickly adapted into money-making movies during the decade. **Photo reproduced by permission of the Corbis Corporation.**

Barbara Kruger (1945–) In the late 1970s, Barbara Kruger began using an artistic form that would mark her work throughout the next decade: putting typed messages directly on top of photographs she took from magazines. The combined pictures and words made her work confrontational and political, such as "You are an experiment in terror" placed over a picture of a hand holding an exploding firecracker. Much of her best work had feminist messages. Kruger's art proved popular and easy to sell in the 1980s, and it was quickly adapted to postcards, T-shirts, and posters.

Wynton Marsalis (1961–) Trumpeter Wynton Marsalis caught the jazz world by surprise in the early 1980s with his technical mastery. Skilled in both jazz and classical, a rare musical talent, Marsalis received a recording contract from Columbia Records in 1981 to record music in both styles. He was just twenty years old. Three years later, in 1984, Marsalis became the first musician ever to win Grammy Awards in jazz and classical in the same year. Remarkably, he repeated the following year, becoming the only person in history to have won back-to-back classical and jazz Grammys.

Photo reproduced by permission of AP/Wide World Photos.

Steven Spielberg (1947–) Steven Spielberg was the most important moviemaker in Hollywood in the 1980s. He not only directed some of the decade's biggest movies—*Raiders of the Lost Ark* (1981) and *E.T.: The Extra-Terrestrial* (1982)—but served as producer on others—*Poltergeist* (1982) and *Back to the Future* (1985). In 1985, Spielberg surprised everyone by directing *The Color Purple,* based on Alice Walker's acclaimed novel about the struggles of an African American woman in the rural South. Although some felt the movie was oversimplified, Spielberg won the Director's Guild prize for his effort. *Photo reproduced by permission of Archive Photos, Inc.*

Bruce Springsteen (1949–) In 1984, Bruce Springsteen released *Born in the USA.* The immediate success of the album caught everyone by surprise. Always popular with critics, Springsteen previously had a small fan base. But the album spawned seven top-ten hits and sold fifteen million copies (it became the seventh best-selling album in U.S. history). The accompanying tour took Springsteen around the world to play in stadium-sized venues. Shows typically sold out in minutes. Springsteen, who had made the covers of both *Time* and *Newsweek* in 1975, was featured again on the cover of *Newsweek.* *Photo reproduced by permission of Archive Photos, Inc.*

August Wilson (1945–) August Wilson emerged as the most highly acclaimed new playwright of the 1980s. Audiences and critics were charmed by his keen instinct for character, dialogue, and blues music. They also responded to his subtle handling of racial and political issues. His first three Broadway productions—*Ma Rainey's Black Bottom* (1984), *Fences* (1987), and *Joe Turner's Come and Gone* (1987)—won New York Drama Critics Circle Awards for best drama. *Fences,* which also won a Pulitzer Prize for best drama and a Tony Award, set a new box-office record for nonmusicals. *Photo reproduced by permission of AP/Wide World Photos.*

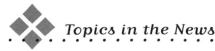

❖ CULTURE WARS: POLITICS VERSUS THE ARTS

The 1960s and 1970s were decades marked by radical social changes in America. Many of those changes were brought about by laws and social programs established by the federal government (and often upheld by the court system). Some Americans believed these changes were good for the country, providing assistance to those who had been less fortunate and a voice to those who had been denied a say in American society. Others believed the changes simply weakened the country, creating a society that depended too heavily on a bloated federal government.

In 1980, the election of Republican Ronald Reagan (1911–) as U.S. president ushered in a federal government that held many strict conservative views. (Conservatives, represented by the Republican Party, favor preserving traditional values and customs. They oppose any sudden change to the arrangement of power in the country, and they believe the federal government should have limited control over the lives of American citizens. On the other hand, liberals, represented by the Democratic Party, favor a stronger central government. They believe in political reforms that extend democracy, distribute wealth more evenly, and bring about social change.) During the decade, those in power in Washington began to question the federal government's increased role in society, especially the government's support of the arts.

The National Endowment for the Arts (NEA) is an independent federal government agency that awards grants to artists and art organizations across the country. In 1989, the NEA's budget came up for review in the U.S. Congress. Many conservative politicians who held strong religious views questioned the NEA's support of artists whose work, they believed, was indecent and irreligious. One such politician was Senator Jesse Helms from North Carolina. He began a drive to ban the NEA or any other federal agency from funding what he termed "obscene" art. Although the U.S. Senate failed to pass Helm's bill, it did cut the funding of the NEA and imposed a five-year ban of federal funding to a few art centers around the country.

Fearful of upsetting conservative politicians and jeopardizing future federal funding of the arts, some art galleries around the country canceled exhibits of and the NEA denied grants to artists whose work was considered controversial. This, in turn, led to protests by other artists who believed that allowing politicians to judge the worthiness of art amounted to censorship and a denial of an artist's First Amendment right to free speech.

Top Films of the 1980s

Year	Film
1980	*The Empire Strikes Back*
1981	*Raiders of the Lost Ark*
1982	*E.T.: The Extra-Terrestrial*
1983	*Return of the Jedi*
1984	*Ghostbusters*
1985	*Back to the Future*
1986	*Top Gun*
1987	*Three Men and a Baby*
1988	*Rain Man*
1989	*Batman*

The NEA and the art world were not the only entities affected by conservative politicians and social groups. Musicians, moviemakers, and writers all faced criticism during the decade from those who believed their work was immoral, irreligious, or unpatriotic. In 1985, the wives of seventeen politicians, including Tipper Gore, the wife of then-Senator Albert Gore, founded the Parents' Music Resource Center. They believed rock music was becoming increasingly violent and sexually explicit. Among other endeavors, the group tried to persuade the music industry to place warning labels on music products deemed inappropriate for younger children.

The movement to ban books from public and school libraries also increased during the decade, with seriously questionable choices. In some communities, groups tried to ban the works of such notable American writers as John Steinbeck (1902–1968) and F. Scott Fitzgerald (1896–1940). In one small Wisconsin town, a group of parents tried to ban *The American Heritage Dictionary* simply because it included words they found objectionable.

❖ THE ART BOOM

The furor over government sponsorship of art in the 1980s did little to stop Americans from investing in art. During the decade, as upper- and

The Satanic Verses

In the fall of 1988, Indian-born English writer Salman Rushdie published *The Satanic Verses*. Little did he or his English publisher know that the book, a work of fiction, would cause such widespread furor that Rushdie would become a household name even to nonreaders. Nor did they realize that for years afterward, Rushdie would live in hiding out of fear for his life.

The Satanic Verses outraged Muslims around the world who were infuriated by what they believed to be insults to their religion. The central belief of Islam (the religious faith of Muslims) is that the archangel Gabriel revealed the word of God to the prophet Muhammad. These messages were later written down to form the Muslim holy book, the Koran. In *The Satanic Verses,* a businessman named Mahound claims access to a rule-making archangel, Gibreel, in order to pass his own laws. The angel's "revelations" become little more than a profitable scam for Mahound. Muslims claimed that through his work, Rushdie not only called into question the validity of the Koran but also repeatedly made irreverent use of sacred names.

Islamic leaders around the world criticized Rushdie, and most Islamic countries banned the book. Publication of the book was postponed or canceled in France, West Germany, Greece, and Turkey. In England, protesters

middle-class Americans became wealthier, they bought more and more art. Consequently, the art market grew tremendously, particularly in New York City. Between 1983 and 1985, more than one hundred galleries opened in New York, seventy-eight of them in the East Village.

As the demand for art increased, so did the price. Gallery sales in 1984 alone exceeded one billion dollars. That year, 50 percent of all art sales were under $1,000; four years later, the average price paid for a work of art had risen to between $7,000 and $11,000. Top auction prices for single works, paid mostly by dealers, hovered at about $3 million early in the decade. By the end of the 1980s, more and more private bidders bypassed dealers to bid on artworks directly. The prices they paid were ten to twenty times the amount dealers had paid only a few years before. Sales at each of the two biggest New York auction houses, Sotheby's and Christie's, surpassed $1 billion in 1987, accounting for a third of the world's art sales.

burned it. Riots took place in India, Pakistan, and South Africa, in which a number of people were killed or injured. Charging Rushdie with blasphemy (disrespect for God or sacred things), Iranian leader Ayatollah Ruhollah Khomeini proclaimed that the author and his publisher should be executed. Multimillion dollar bounties were offered to anyone who could carry out this decree. This *fatwa* or death sentence was reaffirmed by the Iranian government as late as 1993.

In the West, particularly in America, there was a different kind of outrage. Government leaders considered sanctions against Iran. Most political leaders believed Khomeini was using the Rushdie incident as a means of rallying his forces against the West. Meanwhile, American writers joined forces to protect the Iranian leader's actions, signing petitions and organizing speeches, demonstrations, and readings of *The Satanic Verses*. They also forced American booksellers who had removed the novel from their shelves out of fear of terrorist actions to begin selling it again.

The publicity generated by Khomeini's death threat catapulted *The Satanic Verses* onto the best-seller lists. Within a few weeks after the death threat was announced, the first American printing had sold out, and bookstores had received advanced orders for two hundred thousand more copies.

The often astonishing sums of money collectors spent at art auctions caused a stampede of media coverage. Auctions became gala social events. By 1989, the worldwide cash turnover in the art industry was estimated at $50 billion per year.

This huge increase in art collecting and investing in the decade was caused by a number of factors. Chief among these was a change in the U.S. tax laws, which allowed Americans to accumulate or sell all sorts of items without having to pay high taxes in the process. Perhaps the main factor, and the most troubling one, was a seeming resurgence of upper-class greed. Wealthy Americans, from young urban professionals to corporate executives, began to see art as a commodity or good that could be bought, then resold at a higher value, much like real estate. Many of these young tycoons and overnight millionaires were simply looking for new ways to display their wealth.

Bestselling Fiction of the 1980s

Year	Title	Author
1980	*The Covenant*	James A. Michener
1981	*Noble House*	James Clavell
1982	*E.T.: The Extra-Terrestrial Storybook*	William Kotzwinkle
1983	*Return of the Jedi Storybook*	Joan D. Vinge
1984	*The Talisman*	Stephen King and Peter Straub
1985	*The Mammoth Hunters*	Jean M. Auel
1986	*It*	Stephen King
1987	*The Tommyknockers*	Stephen King
1988	*The Cardinal of the Kremlin*	Tom Clancy
1989	*Clear and Present Danger*	Tom Clancy

A new generation of "star" artists also added to the boom in art sales. Julian Schnabel, Keith Haring, Jean-Michel Basquiat, and other artists who emerged in the 1980s aggressively marketed their work. They actively sought media attention. Their artwork, with imagery derived from the media, pop culture, and subway graffiti, was highly appealing to a generation of young Americans who had money to spend and who wanted something new, hip, and trendy. Many new buyers, including doctors, lawyers, advertising executives, and entrepreneurs, had little or no art background or knowledge. Their interest was based on investment, not on a love of the arts. Regardless of their reasons for buying art, these collectors helped to make the visual arts one of the most vital American cultural forces of the 1980s.

*OPPOSITE PAGE
Michael Crawford as "The Phantom" in a scene from Andrew Lloyd Webber's musical* The Phantom of the Opera. *Reproduced by permission of AP/Wide World Photos.*

❖ THE THEATER BOOM

For most of the 1970s, Broadway was dominated by lackluster performances and the revival of nostalgic old shows. That all changed in the 1980s as Broadway rebounded with bigger shows and bigger stars than it had boasted in years. Production budgets and ticket prices matched the size of those shows. In 1980, the typical cost for mounting a big show was about $1 million. By the end of the decade, the cost had mushroomed to four or five times that amount. The $4-million production cost for the Andrew Lloyd Webber musical *Cats* in 1982 set a Broadway record. Only six years later, his *Phantom of the Opera* cost $8 million.

Theatergoers, who paid about ten dollars for a seat in the mid-1970s, paid between twenty-five and forty-five dollars a ticket for a comparable show in 1983. Such high prices were partly due to the fact that, like the rest of America, theater audiences had more money to spend by the mid-1980s. Yet the greatest single reason for escalating production budgets was skyrocketing labor costs. As ticket prices went up, theater audiences began expecting bigger and better shows for the higher prices they paid. Producers, in turn, scurried to find sure-fire box-office hits, packing their productions with elaborate special effects and eye-popping scenery and costumes.

The Broadway musical found itself revived in the 1980s with lavish productions. If any single force can be credited with that with revival, it would be Andrew Lloyd Webber. The English theatrical composer's *Cats,* which had been a smash hit in London, opened on Broadway in 1982. The musical, a splashy fantasy about the lives of cats based on poems by the American-born English writer T. S. Eliot (1888–1965), had American audiences howling with delight. Critics were not as impressed. Nevertheless, *Cats* went on to became the most successful musical of the 1980s.

A scene from the Tony-winning musical Les Misérables. *Reproduced by permission of Michael Le Poer Trench.*

(The longest-running show ever on Broadway, it closed in September 2000.) Heavy on costumes (glowing cats' eyes), effects (actors catapulting onto the stage, a giant tire ascending like a UFO), and scenery design (burning junkyards and oversized garbage), *Cats* defined the Broadway spectacle in the 1980s. By the end of the decade, the show had grossed almost $700 million.

Other notable musicals of the decade included *Les Misérables* (1987) and *The Phantom of the Opera* (1988). With advance ticket sales of $12 million, *Les Misérables* (1987) became one of the biggest musical hits of the decade and won eight Tony Awards. A melodramatic, big-budget adaptation of the novel by French writer Victor Hugo (1802–1885), *Les Misérables* featured a revolving stage and breathtaking sets. During a climactic number, two giant towers merged to form a barricade heaped with the bodies of rebel students. Lloyd Webber's second musical hit of the decade, *The Phantom of the Opera*, made a Broadway star of Michael Crawford and, like *Cats*, won every Tony Award for which it was eligible. Advance-ticket sales topped $18 million. By 1989, the wait for tickets for the show was as long as eight months. The show itself thrilled crowds with its stunning set design, including an underground lake and a giant tumbling chandelier that swooped over the audience to the stage.

In addition to giant musicals, theatergoers in the 1980s also appreciated dramatic plays with serious and challenging themes. The award-winning works of three playwrights stood out. David Mamet's *Glengarry Glen Ross* (1983) focused on a group of cutthroat real estate agents who would do anything to make a sale, including sell each other out. The play won a Pulitzer Prize and a New York Drama Critics Circle Award. Another play that won a Critics Circle Award was Sam Shepard's *A Lie of the Mind,* (1986) which told the story of two families connected by a violent marriage who struggle to make sense of relationships that become increasingly disturbing and dangerous. Emerging playwright August Wilson, however, captured the most attention with his cycle of dramas. His 1986 play, *Fences*, focused on the bitterness of a former baseball player who was too old to play by the time African Americans were allowed into the major leagues in the late 1940s. The play won not only a Critics Circle Award but a Pulitzer Prize and a Tony Award.

❖ MTV AND THE VIDEO BOOM: NEW WAVE, NEW ROMANTICS, AND HAIRCUT BANDS

The music video, in which short performances accompany and illustrate songs, appeared in the early 1980s, seemingly out of nowhere. It quickly became the most influential art form of the decade. Artistically

Top Television Shows of the 1980s

Year	Show
1980	*Dallas*
1981	*Dallas*
1982	*60 Minutes*
1983	*Dallas*
1984	*Dynasty*
1985	*The Cosby Show*
1986	*The Cosby Show*
1987	*The Cosby Show*
1988	*Roseanne* and *The Cosby Show* (tie)
1989	*Roseanne*

these videos were a mixed lot, ranging from electrifying to boring. Most fell somewhere between these extremes. A typical video was a quirky, dreamlike collection of images (a "mini-movie") designed to illustrate fantasies or approximate the live performances of the artist or band.

The music video singlehandedly brought back to life the slumping recording industry. It revolutionized television, expanded radio formatting, ignited the careers of dozens of unknown music performers, breathed new life into dance and choreography, and created a new interconnection among television, movies, and music.

The earliest videos were often simply concert clips, but several artists, particularly in Europe, were experimenting with different formats by the late 1970s. In Europe, the shortage of radio stations motivated many young musicians to seek alternative ways to gain exposure. They made promotional videotapes, which were then played at discos and on television. In England, David Bowie became a forerunner in the new form. Other musicians, such as new-wave bands of the late 1970s and early 1980s, also embraced the form, even if they had limited money to spend on the production.

The true force behind the 1980s video explosion was Music Television (MTV), which began broadcasting in August 1981. MTV was the brain-

Style Over Substance: Milli Vanilli

With the spectacular success of music videos, the "look" of a band or a singer became as important as the quality or content of a song. Record companies began to sign a host of new recording artists who were highly photogenic but who had little to offer musically. Such was the case with the pop duo Milli Vanilli, made up of Rob Pilatus and Fabrice Morvan. The handsome pair, who sported dreadlocks, were dancers by trade, not singers. Yet their 1989 album, *Girl You Know It's True,* sold more than ten million copies and spawned five top-ten singles. In January 1990, they were award the Grammy for Best New Artist.

Then the truth surfaced. In November 1990, Milli Vanilli producer Frank Farian admitted the pair neither rapped nor sang a word in any of their songs on the album. In their videos and stage shows, they had merely lip-synched. Farian exposed the pair because they insisted on doing their own vocals on their next album. Reaction to the confession was swift. Legions of fans turned their backs on the duo, the media criticized them mercilessly, and the Recording Academy forced them to return their Grammy Award.

In 1992, the pair attempted a comeback with *Rob & Fab,* an album on which they actually sang. It sold just two thousand copies. In the spring of 1998, Pilatus died in a German hotel room from an apparent alcohol-and-drug overdose.

child of former radio-program director Robert Pittman. With the financial backing of Warner Communications and American Express, Pittman created the cable network to reach teenagers and young adults who had grown up with television and rock music. And it worked: 85 percent of the viewers were between the ages of twelve and thirty-four. MTV showed twenty-four hours of nonstop music videos every day, with breaks for rock news, commercials, occasional special programming, and chitchat from the "veejays" (video's equivalent of radio's disc jockeys). Record companies supplied their musicians' videos for free in return for free airplay.

After starting with a relatively small playlist—a few hundred clips, mostly rock—and an equally small operating budget, MTV grew rapidly. Although the company did not turn a profit during its first two years, its reach was impressive. When it started, MTV was shown on three hundred cable outlets reaching more than two million American homes. Two years later, it had grow to include two thousand cable outlets received by more than seventeen million homes. By the end of the decade, it was carried by more than five thousand cable outlets and seen by more than forty-six million viewers. Pittman's slogan for the burgeoning network clearly reflected the desire of its audience: "I want my MTV."

New wave, a pop-driven offshoot of punk, finally broke through to mainstream America in the early 1980s, largely due to MTV. Through video exposure, the slick electronic sound of many new wave bands hit a responsive chord in Americans, whose lives in the early 1980s were already becoming inundated with video games and personal computers.

English bands and artists dubbed "New Romantics" were a movement within new wave. The high gloss and style-over-substance of these bands was appealing to fashion-conscious America in the early 1980s, and MTV embraced these musicians and their arty, often quirky, sound. American viewers who would never otherwise have heard, much less seen, these bands were treated to the moody visuals and fashion-plate looks of Soft Cell, Depeche Mode, Orchestral Maneuvers in the Dark (O.M.D.), Adam Ant, ABC, Haircut 100, A Flock of Seagulls, The Fixx, Talk Talk, and others. Not surprisingly, American bands such as The Romantics, Oingo Boingo, Romeo Void, and 'Til Tuesday adopted this look and sound.

Pouty makeup, big spiky hairdos, and complicated fashions formed the standard for video style in the 1980s. The one group that met and raised that standard was Duran Duran. The English group owed its musical life to MTV. In 1983, MTV began playing the highly cinematic videos from Duran Duran's 1982 album, *Rio*. Almost overnight, it went platinum. By the end of 1985, thousands of adoring teenage girls were packing American stadiums to see Duran Duran, which had racked up nine top-twenty hits, including "Hungry Like the Wolf" (1983). Their photogenic good looks, high-tech clothes, and impeccable hairstyles aided immeasurably to their success, and it was all seen on MTV.

❖ MICHAEL MANIA AND MADONNA THE IMAGE MASTER

In 1983, a single talent redefined the style, course, and possibilities of music videos: Michael Jackson. That year he released *Thriller* and made recording history. The album spent thirty-seven weeks of 1983 at number one on the *Billboard* album chart. By early 1984, thirty million copies had been sold, and it was still selling at a rate of more than a million copies a week worldwide. At its height, *Thriller* sold a million copies every four

Top Singles of the 1980s

Year	Song	Artist
1980	"Call Me"	Blondie
1981	"Bette Davis Eyes"	Kim Carnes
1982	"Physical"	Olivia Newton-John
1983	"Every Breath You Take"	The Police
1984	"Say Say Say"	Paul McCartney and Michael Jackson
1985	"Careless Whisper"	Wham! featuring George Michael
1986	"That's What Friends Are For"	Dionne and Friends
1987	"Walk Like an Egyptian"	The Bangles
1988	"Faith"	George Michael
1989	"Look Away"	Chicago

days. It spawned a record-setting seven top-ten singles, including the number-one hits "Billie Jean" and "Beat It" in 1983. Jackson also became the first artist in history to top the single and album charts in both traditional pop and black categories, and he was the first artist of the decade to have two songs in the top five at the same time.

Matching the high-tech pop music on the album were Jackson's flashy dance moves in the accompanying videos. He was electrifying. His catlike twirls, spins, glides, and poses were perfectly matched by his vocals featuring gasps, whoops, moans, squeals, pops, and whispers. The video for "Billie Jean" showed both with style, as Jackson danced along a sidewalk whose squares lit from below when he stepped on them. "Beat It" was harder-edged, with Jackson breaking up a street rumble and leading an aggressive and athletic line dance. *Thriller,* which inspired a thirty-minute video on its creation, was the ultimate well-marketed video product. In 1984, Jackson won an unprecedented eight Grammy Awards for *Thriller,* which went on to sell more than forty million copies to become the top-selling album of all time.

By 1984, Jackson was one of the richest men in America and easily one of the most famous. He earned at least $40 million from the sale of *Thriller.* He pocketed another $50 million from the sale of related prod-

Michael Jackson dancing during a performance in 1984. Reproduced by permission of AP/Wide World Photos.

ucts, such as Michael Jackson key chains, duffel bags, pencils, notebooks, caps, posters, T-shirts, and bubble gum cards. All featured the trademark Jackson image: rhinestone gloves, military jackets, red leather. There was even a Michael Jackson doll.

The media covered Jackson's every move. In January 1984, when his hair caught fire during the filming of a Pepsi commercial, the accident made headline news around the world. His lifestyle was equally newsworthy. Countless tabloid stories detailed his friendships with children, his obsession with singer Diana Ross, his "shrine" to actress Elizabeth Taylor, his dream of starring as Peter Pan, his Neverland estate (complete with a petting zoo and a private amusement park), his habit of sleeping in an air-filtered pod, and his fondness for plastic surgery, which made his face seem increasingly feminine and Caucasian. The constant media frenzy over Jackson made it easy to overlook his true significance as the most powerful force in popular music since the 1960s English rock group The Beatles.

One musical artist of the 1980s who welcomed the attention of the media was Madonna. A shrewd businessperson, Madonna became a one-woman conglomerate, largely through her clever use of music video. Her 1983 self-titled debut album was a harmless collection of upbeat dance hits, including "Holiday" and "Burning Up." Madonna's outfits in her videos began a fashion trend imitated by millions of teen and preteen girls: straps, buckles, belts, bootlaces, hair ribbons, and jewelry (especially her trademark crucifixes) worn in complicated layers over junk-store tights, skirts, black bras, and bustiers.

Madonna's 1985 follow-up album, *Like a Virgin,* launched her to superstardom. It featured what became her theme song in the 1980s, "Material Girl." By this time, feminists began to criticize Madonna, claiming her "boy toy" belt buckles and sexy video come-ons were setting the women's movement back twenty years. Madonna stood firm, stating that her performances were merely entertainment and that her complete control and planning of her image, career, product, and sexuality made her an ideal role model for modern young girls, who made up the bulk of her fans. Others claimed her vocals were weak and her dance-pop sound was frivolous. Good or bad, Madonna seemed unfazed by the press. She merely reveled in the attention.

In a span of five years, Madonna racked up a staggering, record-shattering number of consecutive top-five hits: sixteen, including seven number-ones. She wisely mixed catchy dance numbers with ballads. By constantly changing and updating her look, especially in her videos, Madonna was able remain in the media spotlight for the rest of the decade. In 1986, she junked her thrift-shop image and emerged with a toned dancer's body and sleek blonde looks for the video of "Papa Don't Preach" from the album *True Blue.* Madonna then took a break from music, acting in *Shanghai Surprise* (1986) and *Who's That Girl!* (1987). Both films received poor reviews.

However, Madonna's carefully timed absence from music created an audience and media demand that paid off handsomely with the release of

Like a Prayer in 1989. The title video featured a dark-haired Madonna kissing a black Jesus, dancing on a hillside amid burning crosses, and finding stigmata (marks resembling crucifixion wounds) on her hands. Outraged Catholics protested. In response, Pepsi-Cola, which had signed a $5 million deal with Madonna, withdrew a commercial that featured the song in a different context. Madonna kept the money. With typical confidence and business sense, she shrugged off criticisms from the media and feminists. Indeed, by the end of the decade, it was hard to accuse Madonna of anything except being the master of her own incredible wealth and fame.

❖ BREAK DANCING AND RAP HIT THE MAINSTREAM

During the late 1970s, an underground urban movement known as "hip-hop" arose in the South Bronx area of New York City. Encompassing graffiti art, break dancing, rap music, and fashion, hip-hop became the dominant cultural movement of the African American and Hispanic communities in the 1980s. The popularity of hip-hop spread quickly to a mainstream white audience through movies, music videos, radio play, and media coverage. Rap music in particular found a huge interracial audience, and it emerged as one of the most original music forms of the decade.

Break dancing, a mixture of dancing, tumbling, and gymnastics, became one of the predominant dance forms of the 1980s. Incorporating acrobatic moves such as splits, headstands, flips, and handsprings, break-dancers spun on their shoulders, backs, and heads in an often dazzling display of athletics and choreography. Most dancing was competitive and, like rap music, performed by young inner-city males. This dance style began in the late 1970s as a type of mock urban warfare in which members of opposing street gangs, usually Hispanic, tried to "one-up" each other with hot moves. These teenagers started congregating to perform and compete in underground clubs and on street corners, spinning on pieces of linoleum or cardboard boxes to the thunderous beats of boom boxes. In some inner-city schools, breaking started to replace fighting between rival gangs.

The dance form hit the mainstream in 1983 when Rock Steady Crew of New York performed break-dance moves in the hit movie *Flashdance*. Soon break dancing was prominently featured in music videos and television commercials. It was also being taken seriously as a new art form: The San Francisco Ballet opened its 1984 season with a gala featuring forty-six break-dancers, and the 1984 Summer Olympics in Los Angeles featured one hundred break-dancers in the closing ceremony. All this commercial exposure, however, led to a watering-down of the form: Much of the original style and charm of break dancing was soon lost. By mid-decade, with elderly actors break dancing in movies, the dance form seemed merely silly.

April 2, 1988, marked the end of a scratchy old era and the birth of a shiny new one. On that day, for the first time, all the albums on the *Billboard* Hot 200 Albums chart were available on CD (compact disc). This was the beginning of the end for the vinyl LP (long-playing record) as CD sales surpassed vinyl sales for the first time. The first six months of 1989 were even bleaker for the twelve-inch records: Vinyl sales slipped from 15 percent of the total market to just 6 percent, while CDs rose another 38 percent over the previous year. With an increasing number of new releases available only on CD or cassette tape, record stores began dropping LPs and vinyl 45s (singles) from their inventories. Vinyl-record pressing plants closed their doors for good.

The change had happened so quickly—CDs were introduced in late 1982—that it left many music performers, industry leaders, and fans shaking their heads in bewilderment. Yet in an era of stunning technological advancements, from movie special effects and music videos to home computers and VCRs, it was change or die. And the technology of CDs was hard to resist: They were more resistant to warping and scratching, had better sound quality, and held more music than their vinyl predecessors.

Many vinyl fans, however, refused to make the switch to CDs. They believed the new discs were cold and sterile, lacking the friendly appeal and creative packaging of LPs. They missed the liner notes, posters, foldouts, inner sleeves, and other marketing gimmicks that came with LPs. Their resistance helped keep the LP alive, but only for a few more years. By the 1990s, LPs had become a part of recording history.

Rap originated in the early 1970s in the South Bronx, where DJs at parties played riffs from their favorite dance records, creating new sounds by adding drum synthesizers or scratching over them (scratching involved placing the record needle in a record groove and manually turning the disc back and forth in rapid succession). A partner, the MC, would add a rhyming, spoken vocal (a rap) over the mix, often using clever plays on words. While most rappers boasted about their physical prowess and coolness, some early rappers promoted global and racial harmony. Others expressed serious political and social messages, often addressing the effects of racism, poverty, and crime on the African American community.

Rap remained primarily an underground urban style until the mid-1980s, when it exploded into the mainstream with the unexpected popularity of Run-D.M.C. Formed in 1982, the trio released their first record the following year and watched it become the first rap-music gold album (sold more than five hundred thousand copies). Their true breakthrough to a wider commercial audience came in 1986 when they recorded "Walk This Way," a remake of the song by the rock group Aerosmith. The album that featured it, *Raising Hell,* sold more than three million copies and became the first platinum rap album. Inspired by the success of Run-D.M.C., MTV launched a daily *Yo! MTV Raps* program in 1988. It quickly opened the door for other rap artists, including female rappers such as Salt-N-Pepa, MC Lyte, and Queen Latifah.

While some rap songs were lighthearted and fun, rap music became increasingly political as the decade progressed. Sensing that nothing was being done about the rising problems of crime, poverty, drugs, and unemployment in their communities, many rappers openly raged against the police, the federal government, and big corporations. In response, some critics attacked rap music for being violent, racist, sexually explicit, and demeaning to women. The 1989 album *As Nasty As They Wanna Be* by the group 2 Live Crew was declared by a Florida judge to be legally obscene (the ruling was later overturned on appeal). Most rappers responded to such criticism by insisting that they advocated improving black life through empowerment.

❖ CHARITY EVENTS: ROCK TO THE RESCUE

English pop performer Bob Geldof of the 1970s group Boomtown Rats singlehandedly started a craze for "charity rock" in the mid-1980s. In 1984, Geldof became concerned about the conditions in famine-plagued Africa and decided to organize a relief project. Under the umbrella name of Band Aid, a group of well-known English pop and rock performers recorded "Do They Know It's Christmas?" Released during the 1984 holiday season, the song struck chords of sympathy and guilt with English and American listeners. The song went to number one in England and climbed as high as number thirteen in America, selling three million copies. The Band Aid single and a subsequent album raised $11 million in relief funds, but Geldof also achieved something bigger: He raised awareness of the crisis among millions of pop-music fans.

Meanwhile, in America, singer and actor Harry Belafonte had become equally concerned about conditions in Africa. Aware of Geldof's efforts, Belafonte soon enlisted the help of pop stars Lionel Ritchie and Michael Jackson to write a song. Out of their collaboration came "We Are the World," which a collection of American pop and rock stars recorded in

A new breed of independent, career-minded female artists burst onto the Nashville scene in the early 1980s. Leading the way for country music's tough new women was Reba McEntire. Her gutsy, spirited country sound, showcased on her 1984 release, *My Kind of Country,* earned her that year's Country Music Association award for best female vocalist of the year. From 1985 through 1989, she was the top female country artist, with hits such as "Whoever's in New England" (1986) and "What Am I Gonna Do About You" (1987).

Quickly following in her footsteps were Kathy Mattea, Patti Loveless, and Sweethearts of the Rodeo. Rosanne Cash, daughter of country music legend Johnny Cash, was a spiky-haired rebel favorite with a string of big hits, including "Never Be You" (1986) and "If You Change Your Mind" (1988).

However, the most popular country female act that decade was the mother-daughter singing duo The Judds. Naomi and Wynonna Judd made it big in

1984 with "Mama He's Crazy" off their self-titled debut album. By the end of the following year, the album had produced six number-one singles. The Judds stayed on top of the country music charts for the remainder of the decade, selling more than twenty million records and winning over sixty music industry awards, including five Grammy Awards. **Photo reproduced by permission of AP/Wide World Photos.**

January 1985. The song was released in early March under the name of Belafonte's nonprofit relief organization, USA for Africa. The reaction was overwhelming: In just four weeks, "We Are the World" reached number one on the *Billboard* chart, making it the fastest-climbing single of the 1980s. By July, USA for Africa had earned $55 million, which was to be distributed through established relief agencies.

Even as "We Are the World" was dominating radio, Geldof was organizing the rock-concert event of the decade: Live Aid. The concert was the most complicated live broadcast ever attempted: Two simultaneous events were planned, one at Wembley Stadium in London and one at JFK Stadium in Philadelphia. At a cost of $4 million, the sixteen-hour concert was beamed live via fourteen satellites to an estimated billion and a half people around the world. Before the first of some sixty acts ever took the stages on July 13, 1985, Geldof had already raised $7 million in ticket sales and an equal amount for the broadcasting rights. Despite this success, Geldof and his fellow organizers soon faced a massive problem: how to spend the money. Unfortunately, Geldof's organization lacked the knowledge of how to handle relief efforts. After spending $2.7 million on trucks and trailers to transport grain, it discovered that many of the railways and roads in Africa were impassable. It also received very little cooperation from the government in Ethiopia, one of the area's hardest hit by the famine. In the end, 608,000 tons of grain were stranded in African ports, never to reach those in need.

Spurred on by Live Aid and other charitable efforts, country singer Willie Nelson pushed ahead with his own relief project in 1985: Farm Aid. He was quickly joined in his efforts by musicians Neil Young and John

The Live Aid concert stage in 1985. © Jacques M. Chenet/Corbis. Reproduced by permission of the Corbis Corporation.

(Cougar) Mellencamp. Organized to draw attention to the plight of American farmers, the Farm Aid concert was held on September 22, 1985, in Champaign, Illinois, before a crowd of eighty thousand people. The event raised about $10 million. The concert has been held at different locations around the country almost every year since.

Throughout the 1980s, pop and rock musicians recorded songs and played concerts for various causes, including raising awareness about AIDS, the world's shrinking rain forests, Amnesty International (a worldwide organization dedicated to freeing political prisoners), and apartheid (the racially discriminatory social policy of the Republic of South Africa).

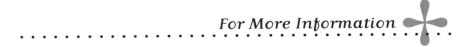

For More Information

BOOKS

George, Nelson. *Hip Hop America.* New York: Penguin, 1999.

Goodwin, Andrew. *Dancing in the Distraction Factory: Music Television and Popular Culture.* Minneapolis: University of Minnesota Press, 1992.

Grant, Adrian. *Michael Jackson: Visual Documentary.* Updated ed. London, England: Music Sales Ltd., 2001.

Metz, Allen, and Carol Benson, eds. *The Madonna Companion: Two Decades of Commentary.* New York: Schirmer Books, 1999.

Rettenmund, Matthew. *Totally Awesome 80s: A Lexicon of the Music, Videos, Movies, TV Shows, Stars, and Trends of That Decadent Decade.* New York: St. Martin's Press, 1996.

Rushdie, Salman. *The Satanic Verses.* New York: Viking Press, 1989.

WEB SITES

Farm Aid: The Official Web Site. http://www.farmaid.org/event/ (accessed on July 29, 2002).

The Grammy Awards. http://www.infoplease.com/ipa/A0150533.html (accessed on July 29, 2002).

Live Aid: A Celebration. http://www.herald.co.uk/local_info/live_aid.html (accessed on July 29, 2002).

National Endowment for the Arts. http://www.herald.co.uk/local_info/live_aid.html (accessed on July 29, 2002).

Welcome to the 80s: The Eighties Nostalgia Site. http://www.inthe80s.com/ (accessed on July 29, 2002).

Yesterdayland—Pop Music in the 80s. http://www.yesterdayland.com/popopedia/shows/decades/music_1980s.php (accessed on July 29, 2002).

chapter two *Business and the Economy*

Chronology

1980: **March** The banking industry is deregulated.

1980: **June** The U.S. Congress passes the Motor Carrier Act, deregulating the trucking industry.

1981: **February 5** President Ronald Reagan makes his first televised address as U.S. president, asking for cuts in the income tax and in government spending.

1981: **March 28** After reaching a high of forty dollars per ounce in January, and a low of four dollars, the price of silver stabilizes at twelve dollars per ounce.

1981: **August 3** Rejecting the terms of a government contract, members of the Professional Air Traffic Controllers Organization go on strike. Two days later, Reagan fires more than eleven thousand air traffic controllers.

1982: The U.S. Congress deregulates the savings and loan industry.

1982: U.S. Secretary of the Interior James Watt opens one billion acres of American coastline to oil and gas drilling.

1982: **July** The U.S. poverty rate is reported at 14 percent, the highest rate since 1967.

1983: **January** U.S. unemployment figures show more than 11.5 million Americans unemployed. By the end of the year, that estimate triples.

1983: **April 20** President Reagan signs Social Security legislation designed to keep the system out of debt for the next seventy-five years.

1983: **November** Drexel Burnham Lambert executive Michael Milken develops the idea of using high-yield "junk" bonds. Many savings and loan institutions begin buying these types of bonds.

1984: The Hewlett-Packard Company introduces the laptop computer.

1984: The computer operating system MS-DOS, developed by the Microsoft Corporation for IBM, is used in two million computers and in more than 90 percent of IBM personal computers and compatible equipment.

1985: A record 43,000 farms go bankrupt as land prices fall and interest rates soar.

1985: Many banks and saving and loan institutions go bankrupt in Texas, Oklahoma, and other oil states that are pressured by collapsing world oil prices.

1985: April 23 Coca-Cola announces that it is replacing its ninety-nine-year-old formula with a sweeter-tasting formula. Protests quickly convince the company to reintroduce the old formula under the name Coca-Cola Classic just a few months later.

1985: September 16 The U.S. Department of Commerce announces that the United States has become a debtor nation for the first time since 1914.

1986: Microsoft Corporation goes public.

1986: The total value of farmland in the United States drops to $392 billion, approximately half its estimated value in 1980.

1986: November 14 Wall Street businessman Ivan Boesky plea bargains with government officials, admitting he had bought stock after receiving tips about forthcoming merger bids. The day becomes known as "Boesky Day" among inside traders.

1987: January The U.S. Commerce Department predicts that technology companies will produce more than other manufacturing companies.

1987: August 10 In one of the largest leveraged buyouts in the decade, the TLC Group acquires Beatrice International Foods for $985 million, making TLC the largest black-owned firm in America.

1987: December The U.S. international debt reaches $368 billion.

1988: The number of millionaires living in the United States rises from 574,000 in 1980 to 1.3 million, and this number includes at least 50 billionaires.

1988: Prices of farmland begin to rise, aiding a recovery in the economy of the Midwest. Large farms begin to replace smaller, family-owned farms.

1988: As saving and loan institutions overextend their credits, experts estimate that $200 billion is needed to bail them out.

1989: January 20 The day George Bush takes the oath of office as president, the national debt stands at $2.68 trillion, more than 2.6 times the figure reported in 1980.

1989: October 31 The first increase in the minimum wage since 1981 is announced. The wage is to rise from $3.35 per hour to $3.80 beginning April 1, 1990.

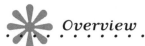 *Overview*

When the 1980s began, many Americans hoped it would be decade of peace and prosperity, quite unlike the decade that had just ended. The 1970s had been filled with tumultuous events, such as oil shortages, the Watergate affair, and the Iran hostage crisis. American businesses also suffered during that decade. The near collapse of the Chrysler Corporation, one of the three large American automobile makers, sent shock waves through an already troubled American economy. A recession, a short decline in economic trade and prosperity, began in 1979 and lasted until 1982.

President Ronald Reagan, elected in 1980, tried to assure the nation that the best course of action to bring about economic recovery was to have the federal government take no decisive action. Instead, Reagan proposed reducing the size of the federal government, reducing taxes, and letting forces in the business world correct economic problems. He tried to restore public confidence in the economy by emphasizing the virtues of American business and the need to take the federal government out of the world of American business.

Reagan and his followers believed in the power of capitalism and the free market, and they worked to remove the federal government from people's lives. This effort took many forms, from deregulation (the lifting of federal regulations on the activities of businesses) to tax cuts for businesses and individuals to lower social spending. Ironically, while the Reagan administration tried to reduce the size of the federal government by cutting social programs, it increased spending for the military dramatically. When Reagan left office in 1989, the national debt (total amount of money owed by the federal government as a result of borrowing) was more than double what it had been when he assumed the presidency eight years earlier.

The "business-first" attitude of the Reagan administration perhaps led to some of the economic excesses and crises of the 1980s. Deregulation of the financial world (and the lack of enforcement of remaining federal regulations) led to disastrous results on Wall Street. The nation was rocked by a series of scandals marked by insider trading, where financiers use illegally obtained information to gain an unfair advantage over their competitors. In some instances, stockbrokers and investment bankers were breaking into the offices of coworkers and rivals to gain information. When the 1980s came to a close, some of the most successful businesspeople of the decade were proven to be criminals.

Deregulation also allowed owners of savings and loan associations to engage in extremely insecure business dealings. Many of those dealings were simply illegal. While the owners made millions of dollars from such activities, people who invested their money in those associations lost everything. The resulting scandal cost the American taxpayers billions of dollars.

Another economic crisis that marked the decade was the one faced by American farmers. Falling land prices and the overproduction of agricultural products had devastating consequences for thousands of small, family-owned farms. Only after the federal government decided to step in did relief come, but for many it was too little and too late.

The one bright spot area on the dreary American economy in the 1980s was the continued rise of the computer industry. Developments in the personal computer, in its hardware and software, opened the computer market to the average American and made fortunes for those behind those developments. It was an industry that would continue to grow and evolve, changing the way Americans conducted business and their personal lives in the decades to come.

Ivan Boesky (1937–) Ivan Boesky was one of the most famous, and notorious, deal makers on Wall Street during the 1980s. However, it was a poorly kept secret that he participated in insider trading. Boesky would use illegally obtained confidential information to gain an unfair advantage in stock trading. In November 1986, government investigators announced that Boesky had pleaded guilty to insider trading and had agreed to pay a $100 million fine. Before he went to jail, Boesky testified against junk bond king Michael Milken and others in the investigation of illegal dealings on Wall Street. *Photo reproduced by permission of the Corbis Corporation.*

Nelson Bunker Hunt (1926–) and William Herbert Hunt (1929–) Nelson Bunker Hunt and his brother William Herbert Hunt attempted one of the most spectacular and unsuccessful financial schemes of the early 1980s. During the 1970s, the Hunts had begun to buy silver, hoping to drive up the price of that precious metal. By 1980, the price had risen from two dollars per ounce to fifty dollars. It was estimated they owned one-third of the world's silver supply. Then, unexpectedly, the value of silver began to fall. The Hunts, who had borrowed heavily to finance their scheme, ended up losing hundreds of millions of dollars. *Photo reproduced by permission of the Corbis Corporation.*

Reginald F. Lewis (1942–1993) Reginald F. Lewis formed TLC Group, a New York investment firm, in 1983. Soon after, the firm acquired the McCall Pattern Company, one of the nation's oldest home sewing pattern companies. In 1987, as chairman of the TLC Group, Lewis sold McCall at an incredible profit over the original purchase price. Using that money, Lewis purchased Beatrice International Foods, an international organization made up of sixty-four companies, for $985 million. The purchase made the new TLC Beatrice the largest African American-led company in America. *Photo reproduced by permission of AP/Wide World Photos.*

Donald Trump (1946–) Donald Trump received more publicity and public acclaim than any other businessperson in the 1980s. In 1975, he had purchased a run-down tract of land near the Hudson River in New York to build a housing development. By the mid-1980s, he had built the Trump Tower, the Trump Plaza, and the Grand Hyatt Hotel. He also moved into the casino business in Atlantic City. Through self-promotion, Trump became a household name in America. In 1987, he published *Trump: The Art of the Deal*, which held up his life as a model for business success. *Photo reproduced by permission of Archive Photos, Inc.*

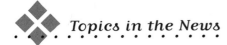

❖ DEREGULATION

The U.S. government, like many other governments around the world, regulates the activity of private businesses in the country. It does so to ensure the health and safety of the workers employed by those businesses. Government regulation also helps control the prices of products and their quality and safety. For example, the federal government regulates the manufacture and sale of many foods and drugs, the production of cars, and the practice of many occupations, including medicine and law. In 1938, to regulate the airline industry, the government created the Civilian Aeronautic Board. It had the authority to establish routes, fares, and safety standards.

In the late 1970s, a movement arose to have the federal government deregulate or reduce the restrictions it had placed on businesses. Many in the movement argued that federal regulations limited business activity, creating economic hardships both for businesses and consumers. When President Jimmy Carter (1924–) was elected in 1976, he promised to free the American people from what many thought was the burden of too much regulation by the U.S. government. By 1980, Carter had begun deregulating airlines, trucking, railroads, and interest rates. However, Carter refused to deregulate federal controls over the environment. In fact, he increased them.

When Republican Ronald Reagan (1911–) assumed the presidency in 1980, the basic framework of deregulation was already in place. Soon, Reagan expanded the scope of the Carter administration's deregulation efforts, removing government controls on many business and decreasing those on telephone, electric, and gas utilities. Reagan then took deregulation even further, focusing on federal agencies such as the Environmental Protection Agency, the Consumer Product Safety Commission, and the Occupational Safety and Health Administration.

Reagan and his administration argued that regulations pertaining to the consumer, the workplace, and the environment were inefficient and expensive. To accommodate businesses, Reagan appointed James Watt as his first secretary of the interior. Watt was a lawyer who had worked for the Mountain States Legal Defense Foundation, an organization that used legal challenges to fight environmental regulations in the West. At the Department of the Interior, Watt reduced or eliminated restrictions on private development of federal lands. Among many other actions, he leased a billion acres of federal land for offshore oil and gas exploration and eased federal restrictions on strip-mining (process of exposing minerals by completely stripping away overlying soil and rocks). Perhaps his most controversial act was to open four California offshore oil tracts for exploration. While Watt was uniformly opposed by environmentalists, his California move drew protests even from leading California Republicans.

By 1985, doubts were rising about the wisdom of deregulation. Without federal regulation of interest rates, it was estimated that several hundred billion dollars in additional interest payments were made by Americans between 1980 and 1988. While the banking industry initially did well in a deregulated economy, other industries did not. The housing industry, which is dependent on borrowing, suffered because of interest rates. Deregulation also influenced air travel. Lower fares and greater competition increased the number of passengers from 297 million in 1980 to over 455 million in 1988. This increase, however, produced complaints about congestion and safety. In addition, because of deregulation, a number of airlines were either bought out by others or forced out of business. This was especially true for small airlines that serviced small towns. By 1988, 140 small towns in America had lost all air service.

Air traffic controllers at work. © Martha Tabor/Working Images Photographs. Reproduced by permission of Martha Tabor.

Average Wages and Cost of Goods: 1985

Median household income	$23,618.00
Minimum wage	$3.35
Cost of an average new home	$100,800.00
Cost of a gallon of regular gas	$1.20
Cost of a first-class stamp	$0.20
Cost of a gallon of milk	$2.26
Cost of a dozen eggs	$0.80
Cost of a loaf of bread	$0.87

After deregulation, financial problems in many industries led to labor strife. From the Reagan administration's point of view, organized labor was another drag on business development. Labor unions in America had enjoyed the right to organize workers since the 1930s, and in the decades since, organized labor had accumulated a good amount of political and economic power. Reagan's attitude toward organized labor was evident when he confronted the Professional Air Traffic Controllers Organization (PATCO) in 1981. In August of that year, PATCO workers went on strike, complaining of stressful working conditions, abusive bosses, and low wages and retirement benefits. Citing a law that bars strikes by federal workers, Reagan fired all of the striking air-traffic controllers. With no sympathy in the administration, organized workers found their position slipping in the 1980s. By the end of the decade, only about 12 percent of American workers in private industry belonged to unions.

❖ THE SAVINGS AND LOAN SCANDAL

The worst result of deregulation by the U.S. government in the 1980s was the savings and loan scandal. In a decade marked by greed, the scandal was monumental. Owners of savings and loans used money invested in their associations by hard-working men and women to fund risky business ventures and lavish lifestyles. In the process, they made millions. In the end, many of the people who invested in the associations lost their all their savings. It is estimated that the cost to U.S. taxpayers to bailout the savings and loan industry will eventually be more than $500 billion. Many believe the scandal is the largest theft ever in history.

Michael Milkin: The Junk Bond King

When a corporation or municipality borrows money from an investor, it gives that investor a bond, which acts like an IOU or promissory note. The bond states the amount of money that will be paid back, when it will be paid back, and how much interest will also be paid on that amount. Junk bonds are given by corporations or municipalities that have a bad credit rating. In exchange for the high risk involved in investing in such a corporation or municipality (the chance that the money might not be paid back), an investor is paid a higher interest rate through the junk bond.

Michael Milken, a financial executive at the Wall Street investment bank Drexel Burnham Lambert, promoted the use of these high-yield junk bonds in the 1980s. Milken and Drexel helped many companies that were just beginning or were small or had a bad credit rating in their business deals by providing the financial backing for their junk bonds. By doing so, they raise millions of dollars in capital for these companies. Junk bonds helped fuel new ventures such as MCI and Turner Broadcasting, but also helped destroy established corporations by funding corporate raiders (companies or people who try to take control of a business by purchasing a substantial amount of its stocks).

In the process, Drexel and Milken made millions of dollars. In 1987, it was reported that Milken earned $550 million himself. However, in September 1988, the U.S. Securities and Exchange Commission (SEC), which oversees the securities markets, filed a lawsuit against Drexel, naming Milken in two counts of insider trading. These charges stemmed from the SEC's investi-

gation of Wall Street trader Ivan Boesky. Milken eventually faced ninety-eight charges, including insider trading, price manipulation, falsifying records, racketeering, and defrauding customers. In the end, Milken pleaded guilty to six relatively minor securities violations. He was fined $600 million, sentenced to prison for ten years (he served twenty-two months), and barred from the securities industry for life. *Photo reproduced by permission of the Corbis Corporation.*

Savings and loan associations are financial institutions that were originally founded in the early 1830s to accept savings from individuals and to reinvest those funds primarily in home mortgages. Although similar to banks, savings and loan associations served a different body of customers. They made most of their money by providing services to working-class and middle-class people rather than to large businesses or other financial institutions.

The first great banking crisis of the twentieth century arose as the American financial system started collapsing in one of the early symptoms of the Great Depression, the period of severe economic decline that began in the United States in 1929. To prevent a similar collapse in the future and to restore the public's confidence in the banking system, the administration of President Franklin D. Roosevelt (1882–1945) established extensive federal regulations controlling banks and other financial institutions. Among these actions was the creation of the Federal Savings and Loan Insurance Corporation, which was to insure all deposits in savings and loan associations.

In the early 1980s, the administration of President Ronald Reagan (1911–) deregulated or removed many of the federal regulations on the banking industry. Savings and loan associations were allowed to offer a much wider set of services, including commercial lending and nonmortgage customer lending. Another change was the raising of the federal insurance on savings and loan deposits from forty thousand dollars to one hundred thousand dollars. At the time, the typical saving account in savings and loan association was only six thousand dollars.

Charles Keating testifying in Washington, D.C., in 1989. Reproduced by permission of AP/Wide World Photos.

In 1982, the U.S. Congress passed the Garn-St. Germain Act, which gave savings and loan associations the liberty to invest their funds more freely. It gave these associations the right to make unsecure and often risky loans to businesses and others, and it gave business developers the right to own savings and loan associations. Perhaps most damaging, it gave savings and loan owners the right to borrow from their own association. They had the power to lend money to themselves.

Unregulated, savings and loan owners made extremely bad investments and poor loan choices. Many invested 100 percent in commercial real estate ventures without asking for any money to be put down by the developers involved. Others invested the money of their association's members in risky deals with businesses that had no credit rating or that had a bad credit rating. And some, like Charles Keating of the Lincoln Savings and Loan in California, used association funds to support a lifestyle that included multimillion-dollar homes, trips to Europe, expensive dinner parties, and excessive salaries, often in the tens of millions of dollars. Keating also used his political clout to try to sway important senators and other Washington politicians on his behalf when federal investigators began to examine his business activities.

As risky business deals fell through, savings and loan associations lost all of the money of their members. In the 1980s, more than five hundred savings and loan associations were forced to file for bankruptcy and close. Federal investigators turned up mounting evidence of fraud by many association owners. An examination of Keating's dealings turned up false profits, hidden losses, and extensive mismanagement. In 1992, he was convicted of fraud and sentenced to ten years in prison. Less than five years later, an appeals court overturned his conviction.

❖ THE FARM CRISIS

Since the founding of America, farming has always held a special place in the national culture. The romantic image of the farm family working the soil is not the only reason for the prominence of farming in American society. Taken as a whole, agriculture is the nation's largest industry. More people work in businesses related to agriculture than in steel and automobile manufacturing combined. During the 1980s, agriculture accounted for 20 percent of the gross national product (the total value of all good and services produced by a country in a year). Yet, it also faced a serious crisis that decade.

The 1970s had been a boom time for farmers. There was an increase in the demand for agricultural products, both at home and abroad. To meet that demand, U.S. Secretary of Agriculture Earl Butz urged farmers to plant on as much of their land as possible. To increase productivity, farmers bought new farm equipment and more land, taking loans from banks and other financial institutions to do so. Low interest rates at the time made these loans seem like sound investments since farmers expected to make more than enough money from increased sales to pay off the loans quickly.

However, as the 1980s emerged, the bottom began to drop out of American agriculture. American farmers produced more crops in the decade than they could sell. Part of the explanation lay in foreign markets. Many smaller countries that had purchased so many American agricultural products went beyond their borrowing limit, and they were forced to reduce their imports. To make matters even more difficult for the indebted farmers, land prices fell sharply. Low land prices lowered the amount of collateral (property put up as security for a loan) farmers had, making additional loans more expensive. Soaring interest rates further added to that expense.

As a result, family farms went bankrupt. Because they could not pay back their loans, many farmers lost their lands to the financial institutions to which they owed money. Between 1981 and 1987, some 235,000 farms went bankrupt, the worst collapse of farms in the twentieth century. The farm collapse slowed only when the Reagan administration decided in the mid-1980s to support farm incomes through federal farm programs. In 1981, federal support represented slightly more than 25

An Iowa Farm Unity Coalition demonstration in 1983. © Bettmann/Corbis. Reproduced by permission of the Corbis Corporation.

American Nobel Prize Winners in Economics

Year	Economist
1980	Lawrence R. Klein
1981	James Tobin
1982	George J. Stigler
1983	Gerard Debreu
1984	No award given to an American
1985	Franco Modigliani
1986	James M. Buchanan Jr.
1987	Robert M. Solow
1988	No award given to an American
1989	No award given to an American

percent of farmers' income; by 1986, it rose to almost 60 percent. Even with these subsidies, the value of farmland in states such as Illinois, Iowa, and Minnesota reached its lowest point in early 1987 before it finally began to recover.

❖ SILICON VALLEY AND THE NEW AMERICAN REVOLUTION

During the 1970s and 1980s, the computer industry and the various industries that produced computer-related materials began to alter American society, changing how and where people worked. Originally, the computer industry was dominated by International Business Machines (IBM). IBM specialized in manufacturing mainframe computers, those that were as big as a room and that required specially trained employees to program and enter data through punch cards. IBM intended for those computers to last for decades, and it believed it would make the most profit not through the initial sale of a mainframe computer but through its continued servicing.

IBM's dominance of the computer market soon caught the attention of the U.S. government, which frowned upon it. To increase competitiveness and development in the market, the U.S. Justice Department brought an antimonopoly suit against IBM, intending to break the company up into a

During the 1980s, Sam Walton (1918–1992) became America's richest man, combining innovation, business savvy, and a down-home style to achieve his success. Walton built his chain of discount stores, Wal-Mart, into the largest in the country, surpassing even K-Mart.

After World War II (1939–45), Walton purchased the franchise of Ben Franklin a five-and-dime store in Newport, Arkansas. In the 1950s, Walton began thinking of owning a chain of stores. The Ben Franklin stores specialized in rural markets, and after some success at running several franchises, Walton proposed that the Ben Franklin stores enter the urban market as a discount chain. The company rejected his proposal, but Walton remained determined. In 1962, he left the Ben Franklin stores and began his own discount store, Wal-Mart.

By 1985, Wal-Mart had more than 750 stores and more than 80,000 employees; five years later, the company had grown to more than 250,000 employees. Walton encouraged change and relied upon input from his employees to further productivity. By the end of the 1980s, Wal-Mart was growing faster and earning greater profits than Sears and K-Mart. In 1983, Walton had also introduced a new membership-only warehouse chain called Sam's Club that brought in $96 billion in annual sales by the end of the decade. In 1990, Walton's personal fortune was estimated to be between $9 and $13 billion.

set of small companies. The suit, costing millions of dollars, dragged on for more than a decade before it was settled in 1982. Under the agreement, IBM ended its practice of discouraging customers from buying competitive systems. IBM also agreed to provide competitors with technical specifications since IBM products often set the standard in the industry. Significantly, IBM also agreed to sell its software as a separate item rather than making it part of the price of the computer. This opened the door for dramatic growth in the software business.

During the 1980s there was an explosion in the sale and development of microcomputers. These personal computers, based on microprocessors, eventually made the mainframe all but obsolete. Apple Computer, formed by Steven Jobs and Steve Wozniak, first introduced the easy-to-use personal computer in the late 1970s and was soon followed into the business by other companies. When IBM entered the market, the company did so in a big way, using its vast resources and name recognition to dominate the personal computer market. In 1980, IBM asked Bill Gates of the newly formed Microsoft Corporation to design an operating system for their new personal computer. That text-based operating system software program, introduced on IBM computers the following year, was known as Disk Operating System or DOS.

The problem with DOS was that it was complicated to use. Only people who had a lot of training and experience with the technology could use it successfully. In 1985, to solve this problem, Microsoft introduced Windows, a graphical operating system for IBM personal computers that provided the ease of use first introduced by Apple with the Macintosh, in 1984. Microsoft and Windows soon came to dominate the software market. IBM, however, lost its dominance in the computer market because, initially, it did not manufacture computers. It merely bought computers from other manufacturers and applied the IBM name to them. Since IBM did not have a patent on the "body" of the computer (the hardware or visible components), other companies were able to copy IBM computers. This led to the term "IBM clone" to describe computers that had the same hardware components as IBM computers and that used DOS and then Windows as the operating system.

During much of the 1980s, the entrepreneurial spirit was still alive in the computer industry as people founded both hardware and software companies. Fred Gibbons founded the Software Publishing Corporation in 1981; by 1985, he had 6 percent of the $400 billion software business. The Intel Corporation, founded in 1968 by Andrew Grove, Gordon Moore, and Robert Noyce, remained a leading developer and manufacturer of microprocessors throughout the decade. J. Reid Anderson's Verbatim Corporation did well selling magnetic storage media, including floppy disks.

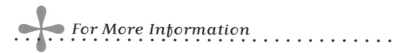

For More Information

BOOKS

Binstein, Michael, and Charles Bowden. *Trust Me: Charles Keating and the Missing Billions.* New York: Random House, 1993.

Carroll, Paul. *Big Blues: The Unmaking of IBM.* New York: Crown, 1993.

Davidson, Osha Gray. *Broken Heartland: The Rise of America's Rural Ghetto.* Expanded ed. Iowa City: University of Iowa Press, 1996.

Ortega, Bob. *In Sam We Trust: The Untold Story of Sam Walton and Wal-Mart, the World's Most Powerful Retailer.* New York: Times Books, 2000.

Pendergrast, Mark. *For God, Country, and Coca-Cola: The Definitive History of the Great American Soft Drink and the Company That Makes It.* Second ed. New York: Basic Books, 2000.

Trump, Donald, with Tony Schwartz. *Trump: The Art of the Deal.* New York: Random House, 1987.

WEB SITES

Computer History Museum. http://www.computerhistory.org/ (accessed on July 29, 2002).

FDIC: Federal Deposit Insurance Corporation. http://www.fdic.gov/ (accessed on July 29, 2002).

FDIC: The S&L Crisis: A Chrono-Bibliography. http://www.fdic.gov/bank/historical/s&l/ (accessed on July 29, 2002).

Nobel e-Museum. http://www.nobel.se/index.html (accessed on July 29, 2002).

U.S. Department of Labor Home Page. http://www.dol.gov/ (accessed on July 29, 2002).

chapter three *Education*

1980: A Gallup poll shows parents believe the three worst problems in the nation's schools are discipline, drug use, and poor curriculum.

1980: **September** One million fewer American children begin kindergarten than in 1979.

1981: The administration of President Ronald Reagan tries to alter the nutritional requirements of school-lunch programs, including defining ketchup and pickle relish as vegetables.

1981: **January** A U.S. Circuit Court of Appeals rules that the First Amendment to the U.S. Constitution "does not require or even allow" public school officials to permit student prayer meetings in classrooms before school.

1982: **August 10** A federal judge throws out a Louisiana creationism suit saying it had no place in federal courts; the Louisiana law required balanced treatment between the teaching of creation science and evolution science in the classroom.

1982: **September** The National Assessment of Educational Progress announces that in five years Hispanic nine-year-olds have made improvements in their reading skills at a level twice the average for children that age.

1983: **July 11** The U.S. Supreme Court upholds a ban on sweep searches of students by dogs.

1983: **November 21** In the first such case in Wisconsin, a teacher is awarded $23,000 in punitive damages from a student who hit him three times in the face.

1984: **May 7** Texas repeals its textbook restriction, passed in 1974, requiring evolution to be presented as "only one of several explanations" of how the universe began.

1984: **September 11** Los Angeles school officials report that students are now required to maintain a C average with no failures in order to participate in extracurricular activities.

1984: **December 17** Ten Arkansas teachers sue to block the state from requiring them to take a literacy test and a competency exam in their subject area.

1985: A study reveals that one-third of the nation's teachers report they are uncomfortable using computers; nearly all, however, want more training.

1985: July 8 Research by the Youth Suicide Center states that 11 percent of the nation's high-school seniors have made a suicide attempt sometime in their lives.

1986: In the first federal study of the nation's teachers in fifteen years, the U.S. Department of Education announces that most put in long workweeks, are quite likely to have advanced degrees, and earn an average salary of $22,701 a year. One-third of male teachers and one-fifth of female teachers have a supplementary job.

1986: August 28 Nobel laureates speak out at a news conference against creationism, claiming that to "teach that the statements of Genesis are scientific truths is to deny all the evidence."

1987: June 19 The U.S. Supreme Court rules that a Louisiana state law requiring the teaching of creationism alongside evolutionary theory is unconstitutional.

1987: August 17 Setting what could be a mandate for textbook publishing nationwide, the California Board of Education unanimously passes a measure requiring more facts on religion in history textbooks.

1987: September 28 A Teachers College study finds that U.S. secondary-school students know less about science than their predecessors did in 1970; U.S. students also lag behind their contemporaries in England and Japan.

1988: January 18 The Education Commission of the States releases a survey on illiteracy that claims that the majority of illiterate people in America are white.

1989: February 27 Three out of four American students do not master enough math to cope in college or on the job, reports the National Research Council.

1989: October 23 An annual survey reveals that fewer students are drinking alcohol and using drugs than two years ago, but more are smoking cigarettes.

1989: December The American Institute for Research announces that forty-four states are now requiring teachers to pass competency tests, up from just ten in 1980.

Overview . . . .

The course education in America took in the 1980s was through a battle-field. Student scores on the Scholastic Aptitude Test (SAT; the measure by which most colleges evaluated applicants) had been on a downward spiral since 1962. That trend continued at the beginning of the decade. Studies showed that American elementary and secondary students consistently tested lower in science and math than their counterparts in Japan, and in what was then West Germany and the former Soviet Union. Evidence was clear that students were learning less in school environments filled with rising drug use and violence.

Democratic and Republican politicians agreed that the nation's schools were not delivering a quality education, but they could not agree on how the U.S. government should act to solve the problem. The admin-istration of President Ronald Reagan wanted to remove the federal govern-ment's presence from education. He and other Republican leaders also wanted to eliminate the U.S. Department of Education. Democrats coun-tered that the continued role of government behind programs such as bilingual education was important for the nation as a whole.

Most education critics agreed the quality of education began to suffer in the 1970s when colleges lowered their entrance requirements and most high schools abolished strict course requirements. The common curricu-lum was lost when an array of electives replaced more academic courses in science, math, and English. High-school curricula, packed with courses such as values education, moral education, death education, consumer education, drug education, and driver education, failed to emphasize fun-damental academic skills.

Many parents and politicians, angered over the state of education, pointed a collective finger at teachers. Even professional education organizations admitted teachers had a problem. Because of low pay and little professional esteem, the teaching field was drawing fewer and fewer quality applicants. Those who did enter the field found their competency questioned by parents and local school boards. Faced with tests to prove their basic abilities in the classroom, many teachers resisted. In the end, the majority of states passed measures requiring such tests. To reward those teachers who demonstrated their worth, school boards decided to establish merit pay systems. Lacking the money to fund such systems, however, many school boards soon abandoned the idea.

Students also were faced with tests. Because the nation began to believe that a high-school diploma no longer represented a level of academic achievement, many school districts adopted minimum competency testing for graduation. In a controversial move, the National Collegiate Athletic Association (NCAA; national organization that administers intercollegiate athletics) adopted Proposition 48 in 1984. This set academic levels that graduating high-school students had to meet in order to participate in collegiate athletic programs.

Perhaps the greatest controversy surrounding education in the 1980s concerned religion in the classroom. Supported by President Reagan, who wanted prayer to be part of the curriculum in all schools, some parents and religious groups fought to change the textbooks used by students nationwide. They filed lawsuit after lawsuit, hoping to have their religious views adopted in place of established scientific and historical information. In almost every occurrence, the courts eventually ruled against them.

William J. Bennett (1943–) William J. Bennett served as the U.S. secretary of education from 1985 to 1989. In that position, Bennett argued strongly that while reading, writing, and arithmetic were important, American schools needed to pay greater attention to the three "Cs": content, character, and choice. He believed that schools should teach children challenging material (content), that educators should set strong moral examples (character), and that parents must have the right to send their children to the school that would provide this type of education (choice). Although controversial, Bennett's educational agenda was popular with many Americans. *Photo reproduced by permission of the Corbis Corporation.*

Allan Bloom (1930–1993) Allan Bloom, professor of political philosophy at the University of Chicago, published *The Closing of the American Mind* in 1987. A best-seller, it ignited a controversy about higher education that lasted for months. In the book, Bloom criticized American universities, saying they had abandoned traditional educational approaches in favor of programs that catered to the demands of women, minorities, and trendy ideas. While some educators and critics agreed with Bloom, many labeled his ideas racist, sexist, misguided, and outdated. *Photo reproduced by permission of AP/Wide World Photos.*

Joe Louis Clark (1939–) High-school principal Joe Louis Clark became a nationwide folk hero in the 1980s when national news reports showed him patrolling the halls of his inner-city high school with a bullhorn and a baseball bat in hand. Clark's tough approach to order, including expelling failing students he believed did not deserve a diploma, angered some teachers and school-board members in his district. However, after six years under his leadership, the school was orderly and student scores on proficiency exams improved. Both students and parents praised his efforts. *Photo reproduced by permission of AP/Wide World Photos.*

Jaime Escalante (1930–) Jaime Escalante challenged his mostly Hispanic students at one of Los Angeles's poorest urban high schools to reach their full potential. Under his tutelage, students were able to pass the difficult Advanced Placement (AP) exam in calculus, which enabled them to receive college credit for classes they had taken in high school. Many of these students went on to receive college degrees from University of California campuses and Ivy League schools. In 1988, the popular film *Stand and Deliver* retold the achievements of Escalante and his students. *Photo reproduced by permission of Arte Publico Press, University of Houston.*

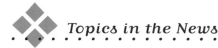

❖ TEACHERS UNDER FIRE

Four independent education studies released by 1984 confirmed what many Americans already knew: The teaching profession was in trouble and getting worse. Part of the problem was a drastically reduced pool of students going into the profession. In 1973, two hundred thousand high-school graduates planned to go into the field. A decade later, just over half of that number of students planned to study to become teachers. Falling salaries might have been one of the reasons behind the decline. In the early 1980s, starting teachers made only thirteen thousand dollars a year, compared to seventeen thousand for beginning accountants. Newly opened opportunities in the business world for women, who traditionally dominated the teaching field, drew away some of the best and the brightest for higher-paying careers.

The studies also indicated that poor teachers led classes in schools across America. Because school administrators feared lawsuits, incompetent teachers were rarely fired in any state in the country. Most alarming was the report that many good teachers were leaving the profession, fed up with hard work for low pay and low prestige. Many were especially upset with the recent trend of testing teachers for basic academic competency.

The American public demanded accountability from the nation's teachers. Since competency testing had been instituted for many high-school students as a standard for graduation, many state legislatures decided that teachers should be similarly tested. Although teacher groups vigorously opposed instituting tests for practicing teachers, they did support testing beginning teachers in basic areas. Politicians and others countered that such tests would not measure the important aspects of teaching: the abilities to maintain order, to inspire students, or to communicate effectively.

In 1983, teacher-competency tests given in thirty-six states produced some embarrassing results. In Houston, where practicing teachers were tested, 62 percent of teachers failed the reading segment, 46 percent failed math, and some tests had to be declared invalid because of cheating. By 1986, forty-two states required competency testing of future teachers.

To reinvigorate the teaching profession, there was widespread agreement that students in teacher training should take more courses in their subject areas and fewer in education. By the end of the decade, this idea was widely accepted by many universities as the basic model for training teachers. Another popular idea was to keep good teachers in the classrooms by designating them "master teachers," a category that would finan-

Grades K-8	27,034,000
Grades 9-12	12,388,000
Total	39,422,000

cially reward excellence, not just experience. Plans for master teacher status or merit pay increases were considered by a majority of the states. Typical plans offered annual salary increases of $1,000 to $7,000 to teachers based on an evaluation of their performance.

While many of these plans were hailed as ideal, they were also deemed impossible. The 1980s was a decade of tight financial budgets for most states, and the amount of money required to meet the merit increases was simply not available. Yet another problem was the inability of school administrators and teachers to agree on guidelines for the required evaluations. Although some states instituted merit pay schemes for teachers, the vast majority of these schemes were abandoned by the end of the decade.

❖ THE RISE IN CENSORSHIP

During his campaign for president in 1980, Ronald Reagan (1911–) told a religious group in Dallas, Texas, there were "great flaws" in the theory of evolution, and he suggested that along with the scientific version of creation, public schools should teach the biblical story of creation. Not surprisingly, after he was elected there was a significant rise in the number of objections to textbooks and curriculum nationwide. In fact, attempts to censor books tripled in the 1980s over the previous decade. Numerous efforts were made to censor classes, textbooks, and library books. Literature classes were the most frequent targets, followed by science, health, sex education, and drug education classes. These censorship attempts were made primarily by religious groups.

In the 1980s, parents who held strong religious convictions filed many lawsuits against the textbooks their children studied in school. Of these, two stand out as representative of the attacks on school textbooks: *Mozert* v. *Hawkins County Public Schools* and *Smith* v. *Board of School Commissioners of Mobile County.*

Replacing the Canon

The literary canon is a name given to a body of works that are considered in some way superior, central, or most worthy of study in a culture. Traditionally, in Western culture these works have been those of Western European writers and thinkers, including ancient Greek poet Homer (eighth century B.C.), Greek philosopher Plato (c. 428–347 B.C.), Italian poet Dante (1265–1321), and English dramatist and poet William Shakespeare (1564–1616).

In the 1980s, many students on college and university campuses across America began to protest against required courses in which only the works of writers in the traditional literary canon were taught. The students claimed that these courses, which were called core courses because it was believed they formed the basis of a college education, disregarded the works of women, minorities, and others. Because they did so, the students argued, the courses were racist, sexist, and elitist.

In the spring of 1986, a small but vocal group of students at Stanford University in California occupied the university president's office for five hours, demanding the university eliminate a required freshman course called Western Culture. The debate over the course continued until 1988, when the university decided to replace the Western Culture course with one called Culture, Ideas, and Values. In the old course, the reading list consisted of fifteen books of Western philosophy and literature. Under the new course, individual instructors had the right to decide the new content yearly, including works by women and minorities in the reading list.

In the decade, Stanford became one of hundreds of colleges and universities that reconsidered the literary canon, broadening traditional courses to include formerly overlooked thinkers and writers.

In the Mozert trial, parents who brought the suit charged that the use of certain textbooks promoted values that were offensive to their religious beliefs. They were especially upset with any textbook containing stories that encouraged the process of imagination. Through their lawsuit, they sought to establish the right for all students to receive individual instruction that conformed to their religious beliefs. While the Tennessee judge ruled in favor of the parents, the U.S. Court of Appeals for the Sixth Circuit rejected that ruling. The appeals court stated that the U.S. Constitution does not require school curricula to be changed in order to accommodate religious beliefs.

In the Smith trial, parents and the religious groups that funded their effort sought to ban forty-five different elementary and high-school textbooks used in social studies, history, and home economics courses. They pointed out that the books made no mention of the beliefs of organized religion. Instead, the books promoted ideas such as a positive self-image, decision making, and personal responsibility. The parents argued that these ideas are part of secular humanism, a philosophy that stresses human values without reference to religion or spirituality. They wanted the court to declare that secular humanism was actually a religion and its ideas should be either removed from textbooks entirely or balanced by the inclusion of Christian teachings. The original court hearing the lawsuit in Alabama decided in favor of the parents, but, as in the Mozert case, the local appeals court overturned that ruling. The appeals court decided that the textbooks promoted important social values such as tolerance and self-respect that neither encouraged nor discouraged any religious beliefs.

Objections to reading material in schools were not limited to religious issues during the decade. Works by many heralded American writers were challenged. In 1985, *Huckleberry Finn,* written by Mark Twain (pseudonym of Samuel Langhorne Clemens, [1835–1910]), became the subject of intense controversy over perceived racism in the novel. A group of African American parents in Illinois, led by educator John H. Wallace, succeeded in having the book taken off the required reading list in local schools. They argued that the book, a classic narrative about the friendship between runaway Huck and runaway slave Jim, should not be taught in schools because characters in the book casually utter racist remarks and frequently use a derogatory term to describe African Americans. Although many literary scholars defended the work, a significant number of school officials across the country followed suit, banning *Huckleberry Finn* from their required curriculum (though not from their library collections). The debate over the place of the novel in classrooms continued into the 1990s.

Perhaps the most controversial issue surrounding censorship in the 1980s was the debate between the teaching of evolution and creationism. The modern theory of evolution, as proposed by English naturalist Charles Darwin (1809–1882), holds that present-day life on Earth evolved from previously existing life-forms through a process of gradual, continuous change over millions of years. Almost all scientists consider evolution one of the most fundamental and most important general concepts in all of the biological sciences. Creationism is a theory about the origin of the universe

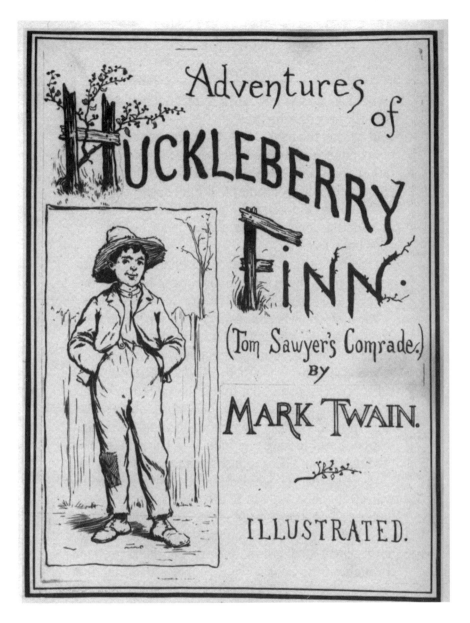

A cover drawing for the first edition of Mark Twain's Adventures of Huckleberry Finn, *which became the subject of censorship in 1985.*

and all life in it, based on the account of creation given in the Old Testament of the Bible. Creationism holds that Earth is probably less than ten thousand years old, that its physical features such as mountains and oceans were created as a result of sudden calamities, and that all life on the planet was miraculously created as it exists today. Because creationism is not based on any presently held scientific principles, members of the scientific community dismiss it as a possible theory of how the universe was created.

Spurred on by the remarks Reagan made during his campaign and by his push for a constitutional amendment authorizing school prayer during his first term as president, religious groups argued that teaching the theory of evolution as fact violated their religious rights. In the many lawsuits they filed during the decade, they maintained that evolution should be taught in sciences classes only if creationism is also taught as another possible explanation for the origin of life.

Scientists responded to these claims by pointing out that a scientific theory is not just any unproven idea: It is a hypothesis that has been backed by empirical results (those derived from observations or experiments) and is subject to further testing. Evolution, they said, has withstood so many tests that virtually the entire scientific community accepts it. Creationism, on the other hand, is a religious belief that is not subject to testing. Therefore, scientists argued, giving equal weight to each in science textbooks would be misleading.

Although the courts almost unanimously sided with the view of scientists in the debate, the decision to teach evolution as the only scientific theory of human origins was made by someone else. In 1984, the Texas Board of Education voted to repeal a ten-year rule restricting the teaching of evolution. Because Texas spent approximately $65 million per year on textbooks (more than 10 percent of the market), publishers hurried to fit the new Texas standards not only for Texas but for the rest of country, as well. By the end of the 1980s, science textbooks used by students across American explicitly outlined evolutionary theory.

❖ PROPOSITION 48: THE PUSH FOR THE STUDENT-ATHLETE

In 1984, prominent Texas business executive H. Ross Perot began a campaign in his state to bar failing high-school students from participating in sports. Perot's reform efforts were successful, and the following year the Texas legislature passed a law requiring students to achieve a 70-percent average in every course for six weeks in order to be eligible to play a sport. Other states around the nation quickly adopted similar measures.

A research study conducted three years later concluded that the Texas law was succeeding. The percentage of students failing dropped from 15.5 in 1984 and 1985 to 12.8 in 1987 and 1988. Although opponents had predicted that students would opt for the easiest courses in the curriculum to assure sports eligibility, the number of athletes enrolled in honors courses remained constant. Also, most students interviewed for the study said the rule encouraged them to achieve.

In 1984, the National Collegiate Athletic Association (NCAA) voted to establish minimum eligibility requirements for freshmen college athletes based on standardized test scores and to implement drug testing at championship events. Student-athletes applying to universities with large athletic departments (Division I and II schools) had to score the following on national college admission examinations: seven hundred on the Scholastic Aptitude Test (SAT) or fifteen on the American College Test (ACT). They also had to have maintained a minimum GPA of 2.0 or better in at least eleven courses in core subjects in high school. These new NCAA rules were called Proposition 48.

Many college and university coaches and athletic directors applauded Proposition 48, believing the rules would benefit all student-athletes by forcing high schools to pay more attention to academics. However, some coaches and others were critical. One of the most outspoken opponents of this new rule was John Thompson, Georgetown University's African American basketball coach. Thompson admitted that some athletes were unprepared for college, but he complained bitterly that the new rules would mainly harm minority students.

Those who agreed with Thompson criticized the rules on the grounds that standardized tests were culturally biased against African Americans

Proposition 48 requires high-school athletes to maintain at least a 2.0 GPA in order to continue participating in sports. © Bettmann/Corbis. Reproduced by permission of the Corbis Corporation.

and other minorities, many of whom were enrolled in some of America's most troubled urban schools. Statistics from the SAT in 1987 showed the average score for African Americans was 728, just above the 700 level required by Proposition 48. Indeed, after Proposition 48 was enacted, the vast majority of freshmen college football players who were disqualified under the rules were African American. In response, Thompson announced that he would boycott any NCAA-sanctioned Georgetown basketball game until Proposition 48 was changed. His protest soon ended, and Proposition 48 remained in effect, setting a clear standard of academic achievement for high-school athletes.

❖ THE CONTINUING BATTLE OVER BILINGUAL EDUCATION

Hispanic immigrants in an English class. These students are members of a bilingual outreach program in Virginia. © David H. Wells/Corbis. Reproduced by permission of the Corbis Corporation.

In the mid-1970s, the U.S. Supreme Court ruled that non-English-speaking students in American schools have the right to receive schooling in their native language. This ruling marked an official recognition of bilingualism in the United States. Schools were thus required to offer courses that students with limited English-speaking ability could understand. However, during the years following this decision, two

Ethnic Makeup of Public School Students, K to 12: 1985

Ethnicity	Percentage
White	69.6
Black	16.8
Hispanic	10.1
Other	3.5

competing philosophies regarding bilingual education emerged. According to one educational philosophy, the goal of bilingual education was to adapt students as quickly as possible to mainstream American culture. Advocates of this philosophy believed students should be immersed in the English language in short-term bilingual programs so that they may better succeed in other subjects that are taught wholly in English. The competing philosophical view asserted that promoting cultural differences was a valid educational goal. Advocates of this view believed students should be taught all of their subject-matter classes in their native language.

The debate over bilingual education took on greater significance in the 1980s as the percentage of households with Spanish as the primary language grew. The number of Hispanic students who required bilingual instruction in school was estimated to be 3.6 million in 1981. These students progressed through school at an average of two to three levels behind their peers. Clearly, improvements in education for this segment of the population were needed.

The administration of President Ronald Reagan (1911–), however, tried to cut federal funding for bilingual education programs. Reagan and his education officials criticized bilingual programs based on the cultural-difference model, believing they failed to help students enter the larger American culture. Instead, they suggested that all bilingual education programs should follow the short-term immersion model.

In 1988, the National Advisory and Coordinating Council on Bilingual Education released a report to the U.S. Congress on the state of bilingual education in America. The report stated that the quality of student instruction was more important than any particular method or philoso-

Apartheid and Campus Protests

Beginning in the late 1940s, the government of South Africa officially adopted the policy of apartheid (pronounced ah-PART-hite), a system of legal and economic racial discrimination that not only separated whites from nonwhites but also groups of nonwhites from each other. By the 1960s, demonstrations in countries around the world arose against the policy. International religious organizations and even the United Nations voiced opposition to apartheid. Protests organized by churches and students continued throughout the 1970s and 1980s.

In 1985, the administration of President Ronald Reagan defended its refusal to apply economic sanctions against South Africa as a means of ending that country's policy of apartheid. On April 4, 1985, to mark the seventeenth anniversary of the assassination of civil rights leader Martin Luther King Jr. (1929–1968), students on campuses all across the United States demonstrated against racism in general and South Africa's apartheid system in particular. Twenty day later, thousands of students around the country took part in what organizers named National Anti-apartheid Protest Day and A Day of National Solidarity. On many campuses, the students demanded that their university sell any stock it owned in companies that did business in South Africa.

Some universities did agree to rid themselves of any holdings connected with South Africa. In 1985, Stanford University trustees voted to sell the university's five-million-dollar stock investment in Motorola if the company resumed sales of electronic gear to the South African military or police. That same year, Harvard University announced it had sold its stock holdings in Baker International Corporation after the company refused to provide evidence that its South African operations were ethical. Although Harvard had taken an official stand against the apartheid system, this sale was the first time that the university had sold part of its stocks to back up its position.

phy. In some settings, one bilingual instruction approach was more successful; in others, it was not. The best bilingual programs were judged to be those taught by teachers who maintained high expectations of their students while remaining sensitive to their students' linguistic and cultural needs.

U.S. High School Dropout Percentage: 1985

Total, all races	12.6
Total, white	10.4
Total, black	15.2
Total, Hispanic	27.6
Male, all races	13.4
Male, white	11.1
Male, black	16.1
Male, Hispanic	29.9
Female, all races	11.8
Female, white	9.8
Female, black	14.3
Female, Hispanic	25.2

❖ DRUG USE AND VIOLENCE IN SCHOOLS

Throughout the 1980s, newspaper headlines across the country announced shocking occurrences of violence and abuse in the nation's schools. Many of these problems were associated with illegal drugs. In 1979, surveys of student drug use indicated that 54 percent had tried drugs at least once. In annual survey from 1980 to 1987, parents consistently listed drug use as their greatest worry about their children's schools.

To combat the growing drug problem in American schools, First Lady Nancy Reagan started a "Just Say No" campaign in the early 1980s. The targeted audience was elementary-school students. The "Just Say No" program replaced the usual lectures about the dangers of drugs with sports, games, and programs aimed at helping children develop the ability to decline offers from drug dealers. When he became president in 1989, George Bush (1924–) set aside more than $250 million for drug-related programs in the schools. William J. Bennett, President Bush's coordinator of drug policy, warned that schools without valid drug-use policies would not receive federal funding.

These and other programs that stressed the dangers of illegal drugs all seemed to work. By the late 1980s, studies indicated the use of alcohol, marijuana, cocaine, PCP, and other drugs by students appeared to be declining. Only cigarette smoking remained constant, with 29 percent of students reporting regular usage.

Although drug use appeared to wane in the 1980s, violent episodes in the schools, especially those involving guns, increased dramatically. Violence may not have been the norm, but it also was not an isolated problem. In New York City in 1989, metal detectors in only five high schools uncovered more than two hundred guns. At Lindbergh Middle School in Long Beach, California, a ten-foot-high, nine-hundred-foot-long concrete wall was erected between the school and a nearby housing project to protect students from flying bullets. At the end of the decade, the American Federation of Teachers reported that 66 percent of member teachers surveyed were scared of violence and gang activity; more than 70 percent knew colleagues who had been victimized by teens. Teachers attributed the problems to the easy access to guns and drugs, a lack of parental supervision, and the influence of violence in the media.

In this culture of drug use and prevalent violence, suicide attempts by teenagers became all too frequent. Schools reacted by adding suicide prevention information into their curriculums. Teachers' workshops frequently centered on ways to detect potential problems regarding suicidal students. As early as 1982, California became the first state to mandate a state task force to train teachers how to counsel students in the aftermath of suicide attempts by their classmates. Several state departments of education also added a required college course in suicide prevention.

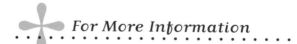 *For More Information*

BOOKS

Bennett, William J. *The De-Valuing of America: The Fight for Our Culture and Our Children.* Nashville, TN: Thomas Nelson, 1994.

Bloom, Alan. *The Closing of the American Mind.* New York: Simon and Schuster, 1987.

Byers, Ann. *Jaime Escalante: Sensational Teacher.* Berkeley Heights, NJ: Enslow Publishers, 1996.

Delfattore, Joan. *What Johnny Shouldn't Read: Textbook Censorship in America.* New Haven, CT: Yale University Press, 1992.

WEB SITES

National Center for Education Statistics Home Page. http://nces.ed.gov/ (accessed on July 29, 2002).

National Clearinghouse for English Language Acquisition and Language Instruction Educational Programs. http://www.ncbe.gwu.edu/index.htm (accessed
on July 29, 2002).

U.S. Department of Education. http://www.ed.gov/index.jsp (accessed on July 29,
2002).

chapter four *Government,*
Politics, and Law

1980: **January 4** President Jimmy Carter reacts to the Soviet Union's invasion of Afghanistan on December 29, 1979, by withdrawing the SALT II arms-control treaty from consideration by the U.S. Senate.

1980: **April 12** At the urging of President Carter, the U.S. Olympic Committee votes to boycott the 1980 Summer Olympics in Moscow to protest the Soviet invasion of Afghanistan.

1981: **March** President Ronald Reagan directs the Central Intelligence Agency (CIA) to assist contra (counterrevolutionary) forces opposed to the Marxist Sandinista government in Nicaragua.

1981: **March 30** John W. Hinckley Jr. shoots Reagan in the chest outside of the Washington Hilton Hotel. Press Secretary James Brady, a Secret Service agent, and a Washington, D.C., police officer are also wounded.

1981: Reagan nominates Sandra Day O'Connor to be the first woman justice on the U.S. Supreme Court.

1982: The United States adopts a Defense Guidance Plan, which outlines a $1.2-trillion increase in defense spending over a five-year period.

1982: **November 13** In Washington, D.C., 150,000 observers witness the dedication of the Vietnam Veterans Memorial.

1982: **December 8** Congressman Edward Boland (D-Mass.) successfully sponsors an amendment making it illegal to use U.S. funds to overthrow the Sandinista government of Nicaragua. Congress renews the amendment in 1983, 1984, and 1985, extending it through the 1986 fiscal year.

1983: **March 23** Reagan proposes the development of a defense shield, at least partly based in space, to intercept incoming missiles. Formally called the Strategic Defense Initiative (SDI), the proposal becomes popularly known as "Star Wars."

1983: **April** The American public learns that the CIA assisted a contra attack on Nicaragua oil terminals.

1984: **April 9** Nicaragua asks the International Court of Justice to rule that U.S. aid to the contra rebels and its role in mining Nicaraguan harbors is illegal. The United States contends the court has no jurisdiction in the matter.

1984: **April 10** The U.S. Senate passes a nonbinding resolution opposing the use of federal funds to mine Nicaraguan harbors. Two days later, the U.S. House of Representatives also approves the resolution.

1985: **Spring** Israeli intelligence tells the United States that Shiite Muslims will exchange western hostages for arms for Iran.

1985: **August** Reagan agrees to ship anti-tank missiles to Iran with the hope of winning the release of American hostages. After the missiles are delivered, only one hostage is released.

1985: **November** At the urging of Lieutenant Colonel Oliver North and with the covert assistance of the CIA, a shipment of Hawk missiles is delivered to Iran.

1986: **November 13** Reagan says the United States has sent Iran a few defensive weapons and spare parts, but he denies any attempt to exchange weapons for hostages.

1986: **November 23** U.S. Attorney General Edwin Meese III announces he has discovered that proceeds from the sale of arms to Iran have been diverted to the contras.

1987: **May 5–August 3** The U.S. Congress holds public hearings on the Iran-Contra scandal.

1987: **October 23** The U.S. Senate rejects the nomination of Robert Bork to the U.S. Supreme Court.

1988: **March 16** A federal grand jury in Washington, D.C., indicts Admiral John Poindexter, Oliver North, and two others on charges relating to their involvement in the Iran-Contra scandal.

1988: **May 27** The U.S. Senate ratifies the Intermediate Nuclear Forces (INF) Treaty, under which the United States and the Soviet Union agree to eliminate intermediate-range weapons from their nuclear arsenals.

1989: **May 4** Oliver North is found guilty on three felony charges: obstructing a congressional inquiry, destroying documents, and accepting an illegal gift.

1989: **December 20** U.S. troops invade Panama and overthrow the government of Manuel Noriega, who surrenders on January 3, 1990, and is extradited to the United States, where he is tried and found guilty on drug-trafficking charges in 1992.

Overview

In American politics, the 1980s was the decade of Ronald Reagan. His vision of the nation and his conservative agenda shaped the economic and political fortunes of the United States throughout the decade and even into the next. Reagan and his administration had a profound influence on the way Americans thought about themselves and the world at large.

From the beginning of his time in office, Reagan conducted foreign policy according to the belief that communism was the enemy and any enemy of communism was a friend of the United States. It mattered little to Reagan or members of his administration if the groups or governments they supported were less than honorable. As long as they were fighting communism, the Reagan administration supplied the money and arms to do so.

Reagan sought to protect the country and destroy communism at the same time by building up the might of the American military. He ordered over $1 trillion in new defense spending and proposed the development of a defense shield around the country, based both on the ground and in space, that would destroy any nuclear missiles launched against the United States. Reagan and his administration believed the shield would allow the nation to retaliate to a nuclear strike and win a nuclear war. Exactly how the space shield would work remained unclear. Many experts believed the science behind the plan was impossible. Others believed the plan was merely science fiction.

The realization of the extremely expensive and technical defense shield proved unnecessary when Mikhail Gorbachev rose to power in the Soviet Union in 1985. Political tensions between the United States and the Soviet Union began to ease, and real progress was made in arms control. Some political historians believe the U.S. military buildup and possible defense shield forced Gorbachev to act, but others claim Gorbachev was a new kind of Soviet leader who had vision and a desire to change his country for the better. His willingness to cut Soviet aid to Third World countries and his withdrawal of Soviet troops from eastern Europe ushered in a major transformation in world politics. By the end of the decade, nearly every communist government in Eastern Europe collapsed and was replaced by a new, democratically elected government.

A champion of the rich and powerful, Reagan wanted to introduce a new economic program to the country that would reward those at the top of the economic ladder. Critics charged that his economic program took from the poor to enrich the wealthy and that the nation he envisioned left out minorities, the disadvantaged, and the disabled. Reagan and his supporters replied that economic incentives to the wealthy would "trickle down" to the rest of America, enriching everyone.

Reagan's economic program never actually worked as planned. Tax-reform bills passed by the U.S. Congress substantially reduced income tax rates for individuals and corporations, but the economy did not grow quickly enough to offset that loss of revenue. Primarily because of major increases in military spending, the federal deficit grew enormously by the end of the decade. Reagan could take credit for strengthening the economy, but the huge deficit marred his economic accomplishments.

Reagan, who was nearly seventy when he took office in January 1981, was the oldest man ever to serve as chief executive. Throughout his presidency, there were frequent jokes about his tendency to fall asleep during cabinet meetings and his apparent ignorance about actions his administration took in his name. The laughter stopped in late 1986 when news of the Iran-Contra scandal surfaced. The nation learned that members of his administration had been illegally selling arms to Iran in return for the release of Americans held hostage by Islamic radicals in the Middle East. The scandal deepened when it was revealed that profits from the arms sales had been diverted to aid rebels fighting the communist government in Nicaragua, an action the U.S. Congress had specifically banned. The scandal tarnished Reagan's image and seriously undermined the effectiveness of his administration at the end of his second term.

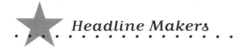

Tawana Brawley (1972–) Tawana Brawley shocked New Yorkers on November 29, 1987, when she claimed she had been brutally raped and abused over a four-day period by six white men, some or all of whom may have been law enforcement officers. Shortly after the apparently racially motivated attack was revealed, several self-appointed advisors, including civil rights leader Al Sharpton, stepped in to assist the Brawley family. They quickly claimed a cover-up was under way to protect the officers involved in the assault. Almost a year later, a grand jury ruled that evidence conclusively proved that Brawley had fabricated the story. *Photo reproduced by permission of AP/Wide World Photos.*

Robert H. Bork (1927–) Robert H. Bork was a respected federal appeals court judge when President Reagan nominated him in 1987 to serve on the U.S. Supreme Court. His nomination, however, went down to defeat when Democrats on the U.S. Senate Judiciary Committee used the unprecedented televised proceedings to bring to light his many conservative opinions. Bork opposed new civil rights laws, abortion, and preferential treatment for minorities and women. To the viewing public, he appeared uncaring and intellectually arrogant. In the end, his nomination to the Supreme Court was denied by the largest margin of all unsuccessful Supreme Court nominees in U.S. history. *Photo reproduced by permission of the Corbis Corporation.*

Geraldine Ferraro (1935–) Geraldine Ferraro served as a Democratic congresswoman from Queens, New York, before Walter Mondale announced on July 12, 1984, that she would be his running mate in the presidential election that fall. With that announcement, Ferraro became the first woman ever to seek the vice presidency as the candidate of a major national political party. Many Democrats hailed her nomination. Her lack of experience in foreign affairs, her stand on abortion, and her husband's questionable financial dealings soon tarnished her image. After she and Mondale lost the November election, she found it hard to re-enter politics. *Photo reproduced by permission of Archive Photos, Inc.*

Bernhard Goetz (1947–) Bernhard Goetz made headlines nationwide when he shot four African American youths on the New York subway on December 22, 1984. One of the youths was paralyzed from the waist down as a result. Goetz, who had been robbed and assaulted in 1981, waited nine days before turning himself in to police. He claimed two of the youths had asked him for five dollars in a threatening manner before he started shooting. Charged with assault, attempted murder, reckless endangerment, and illegal weapons possession, Goetz was found guilty of only the last charge in June 1987. *Photo reproduced by permission of AP/Wide World Photos.*

Jesse Jackson (1941–) Jesse Jackson made history in 1984 when he campaigned to be the Democratic candidate for the presidency of the United States. He was the first African American to wage a full-scale campaign to head a major-party ticket. Although many considered his foreign-policy agenda to be controversial, Jackson finished in third place among the Democratic challengers. Four years later, he made a second run for the office of president, emphasizing the theme of unity. This time, he finished in a strong second place behind Michael Dukakis, the eventual Democratic nominee. *Photo reproduced by permission of the Corbis Corporation.*

Oliver North (1943–) Oliver North gained the most notoriety of all individuals charged in the Iran-Contra scandal. A lieutenant colonel in the U.S. Marine Corps, North worked as a staff assistant to the National Security Council (NSC). The Reagan administration used the NSC to funnel aid to the contra (counterrevolutionary) rebels in Nicaragua. North directed the operation. When his activities were discovered, North was forced to testify before the U.S. Congress. He became a folk hero to many when he contended he was merely a loyal soldier serving his commander in chief, whether or not he violated the U.S. Constitution. *Photo reproduced by permission of Archive Photos, Inc.*

Sandra Day O'Connor (1930–) Sandra Day O'Connor became the first female U.S. Supreme Court justice when the U.S. Senate unanimously confirmed her nomination to the Court on September 26, 1981. Initially thought to be a staunch conservative, she has in fact sided with both conservative and liberal justices on many issues before the Court. No one, however, has ever questioned her commitment. In 1988, O'Connor was diagnosed with breast cancer, underwent surgery, then returned to the Court ten days later, without missing any work. *Photo reproduced by permission of the Corbis Corporation.*

David A. Stockman (1946–) David A. Stockman served in the Reagan administration as the director of the Office of Management and Budget. When he assumed the post in 1981, he was just thirty-four years old. Famous for his vast knowledge of the federal budget and his great desire to cut it, Stockman took the lead in attacking federal government spending. He quickly realized, however, that Reagan's economic agenda had serious miscalculations that would lead to massive deficit spending. Stockman than became openly critical of the president's economic approach. He left the Reagan administration in 1986.

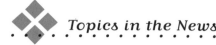

Topics in the News

❖ THE REAGAN ERA: A HARD-LINE APPROACH TO COMMUNISM

During the 1980 presidential campaign, Ronald Reagan (1911–) projected an optimistic, "can-do" attitude. He offered an appealing vision of an America restored to its former glory and prosperity through hard work, self-reliance, and faith in God. He appealed to Americans' deep-seated patriotism with his vow to restore the prestige and power of the United States in foreign policy.

At the top of Reagan's foreign-policy list was the defeat of communism (political system or form of government, such as in China or the former Soviet Union, in which all property and wealth is shared by all members of the community). The creation of the world's first nuclear weapons during World War II (1939–45) had sparked the "Atomic Age," which brought with it new power struggles and a great shift in the political thought of the U.S. government. The United States and the Soviet Union had emerged from the war as the world's two superpowers, and the United States no longer considered the Soviet Union an ally. Instead, a hostile yet nonviolent period of relations, which became known as the Cold War, developed between the two nations, and a far-reaching and rapid campaign against communism was begun in the United States.

To root out communism in American society, the U.S. Congress had begun hearings at which people were called to testify against suspected communists. At the war's end, Reagan had become active in the Screen Actors Guild (SAG), soon serving as its president. Because of his standing in Hollywood, Reagan was called before Congress to testify about possible communists in the movie business. It was from his experience battling alleged communist penetration of SAG that Reagan developed the anticommunist beliefs that would remain at the core of his convictions through his presidency.

During his presidential campaign, Reagan pledged he would confront the Soviet Union and vigorously oppose communism and terrorism everywhere. After winning the presidential election, Reagan continued his anti-Soviet rhetoric. Early in his presidency, he charged that Soviet leaders were capable of lying, cheating, and stealing to further their cause. Speaking to a group of religious broadcasters in March 1983, Reagan referred to the Soviet Union as the "evil empire."

Reagan soon backed his words with deeds. He increased military spending by over $1 trillion, the largest peacetime buildup of the U.S. military in years. He proposed developing a protective shield, partially based in space, to intercept any incoming nuclear missiles from the Soviet Union and others. His administration provided money, arms, and military assistance to anticommunist revolt movements in Angola, Nicaragua, and Afghanistan and anticommunist governments in the Philippines and El Salvador. It did not matter if those governments or movements were guilty of human-rights violations. It also did not matter to the Reagan administration if the U.S. Congress had outlawed such activities.

Reagan committed U.S. troops to assist peacekeeping efforts in Lebanon, ordered the bombing of Libya in retaliation for its support of terrorist activities, and launched an invasion of Grenada to oust a government friendly to Fidel Castro's communist government in Cuba. By authorizing a massive arms buildup and creating a foreign policy based on the belief that a nuclear war in Europe was winnable, Reagan nearly scrapped the policy of détente (pronounced day-TONT; a lessening of hostility or tension between nations) with the Soviet Union that President Richard M. Nixon (1913–1994) had developed nearly a decade before.

❖ THE MILITARY BUILDUP AND "STAR WARS"

To achieve his aim of defeating communism, Ronald Reagan (1911–) increased military spending during his first term as president. It was the

Ronald Reagan and his family at the 1980 Republican National Convention in Detroit. **Reproduced by permission of the Corbis Corporation.**

Presidential Election Results of the 1980s

Presidential Election Results: 1980

Presidential/ Vice Presidential Candidate	Political Party	Popular Vote	Electoral Vote
Ronald Reagan/ George Bush	Republican	43,904,153 (50.75%)	489 (90.9%)
Jimmy Carter/ Walter Mondale	Democrat	35,483,883 (41.01%)	49 (9.1%)
John Anderson/ Patrick Lucey	National Union	5,720,060 (6.61%)	0 (0.0%)
Ed Clark/ David Koch	Libertarian	921,299 (1.06%)	0 (0.0%)
Other		485,826 (0.56%)	0 (0.0%)

Presidential Election Results: 1984

Presidential/ Vice Presidential Candidate	Political Party	Popular Vote	Electoral Vote
Ronald Reagan/ George Bush	Republican	54,455,075 (58.77%)	525 (97.6%)

biggest peacetime buildup since 1940 and the largest in the history of the United States. In 1982, his second year in office, Reagan issued the Defense Guidance Plan, which called for an increase in military spending of $1.2 trillion over five years. Reagan and his administration also wanted to increase the size of the U.S. Navy to six hundred ships.

One of Reagan's more controversial acts in regard to increasing military strength was to revive plans to build the B-1 bomber. President Richard M. Nixon (1913–1994) had proposed the development of the B-1 in 1970. The first supersonic bomber, its primary mission was to deliver nuclear bombs anywhere around the world, including deep inside the Soviet Union. Antiwar protestors heavily criticized the B-1 program during the 1970s, and in 1977, President Jimmy Carter (1924–) canceled the program. Four years later, Reagan restarted it, and the B-1 became the

Walter Mondale/ Geraldine Ferraro	Democrat	37,577,185 (41.03%)	13 (2.4%)
David Bergland/ James Lewis	Libertarian	228,314 (0.24%)	0 (0.0%)
Other		392,268 (0.42%)	0 (0.0%)

Presidential Election Results: 1988

Presidential/ Vice Presidential Candidate	Political Party	Popular Vote	Electoral Vote
George Bush/ J. Danforth Quayle	Republican	48,886,588 (53.37%)	426 (79.2%)
Michael Dukakis/ Lloyd Bentsen	Democrat	41,809,485 (45.65%)	111 (20.6%)
Lloyd Bentsen/ Michael Dukakis	Democrat		1 (0.2%)
Ron Paul/ Andre Marrou	Libertarian	432,184 (0.47%)	0 (0.0%)
Other		467,463 (0.51%)	0 (0.0%)

largest military program at the time. By the time Reagan left office in 1988, one hundred B-1 bombers had been built.

While the B-1 was controversial, Reagan's call for a military system to be used to defend against potential nuclear attack by the Soviet Union both on the ground and in space was almost unimaginable. The threat of nuclear warfare had gripped the world since scientists in the United States created the first atomic bombs in 1945. In 1949, the Soviet Union built its own atomic bomb, and the arms race was on. In the 1950s and 1960s, airplanes were the chosen means to deliver nuclear warheads to their destinations. To guard against Soviet bombers, President Dwight D. Eisenhower (1890–1969) developed an antiaircraft defense system. In the 1960s, with the introduction of the technology of rocketry, the preferred delivery system became the intercontinental ballistic missile (ICBM).

Nancy and Her Astrologer

Ronald and Nancy Reagan had been interested in astrology for many years, a fact he had revealed in his 1965 autobiography, *Where's the Rest of Me?* In the late 1960s, when Reagan was governor of California, Mrs. Reagan even consulted astrologers to help determine his best course of action while in office.

After Reagan was elected U.S. president in 1980, Mrs. Reagan began to consult Joan Quigley, a San Francisco astrologer whom she had met almost a decade before. Her faith in Quigley was reinforced after Quigley had predicted that something bad would happen to the president on March 30, 1981. On that day, John Hinckley Jr. tried to assassinate Reagan when he emerged from the Washington Hilton Hotel after delivering a speech.

Fearing for her husband's safety after this, Mrs. Reagan dictated the president's schedule based on advice from Quigley, whom she called every Saturday, usually from Camp David, the presidential retreat in central Maryland. For the most part, Quigley determined when it was best for Reagan to move from one place to another, to speak in public, or to begin negotiations with foreign leaders. On some occasions, Reagan was not allowed to leave the White House because of predictions by Quigley.

The American public became aware of the great influence of an astrologer on the president's schedule in the spring of 1988 when former White House Chief of Staff Donald Regan revealed so in his memoir, *For the Record*. When the news broke, the president stated emphatically that he had never consulted an astrologer about policy decisions. Although Mrs. Reagan tried to stress that Quigley had only offered advice on scheduling, the damage was done. Quigley was quickly taken off the White House payroll.

The development of ICBMs then led the United States, during President Nixon's administration, to develop antiballistic missiles (ABMs) that could shoot down incoming enemy missiles. The creation of ABMs led both sides to search for further means of delivering their bombs to their targets. As a result, multiple independently targetable reentry vehicles (MIRVs) were created in the 1970s. MIRVs, consisting of one launch rocket with several nuclear bombs aboard, were able to overwhelm ABM defenses. All of these military developments increased the concern that a first nuclear strike by the Soviet Union on the United States (or the reverse) was possible.

As part of an expanded national defense system, the Reagan administration introduced the Strategic Defense Initiative (SDI). It was to make use of the latest technology, and develop new technologies where necessary, in putting into place a protective shield (based both in space and on Earth) around the United States in the event of a Soviet nuclear missile attack. SDI had two essential components: surveillance of Soviet activities so that a launch could be detected at the earliest possible moment and the necessary weaponry to disable Soviet nuclear warheads before they reached the United States. Backers of SDI asserted that it would do what ABMs could not: protect Americans in the event of a nuclear war.

Initial estimates put the project's price at around $30 billion. Experts were soon pointing out that the cost might be as high as $1 trillion. Because SDI was to use lasers, subatomic particle beams, "bullets" launched from electromagnetic rail guns, and other space-age technologies, it was dubbed "Star Wars," after the popular 1977 science-fiction film. By the mid-1980s, the goals of SDI were downsized. Rather than preventing any Soviet missiles from reaching U.S. targets, the new aim was to

A B-1 bomber rolling down a runway. As the first supersonic bomber, its primary mission was to deliver nuclear bombs anywhere around the world. **Reproduced by permission of the Corbis Corporation.**

Ronald Reagan

Ronald Reagan captivated millions of Americans with his ability to communicate the need for values such as patriotism, religion, hard work, and self-reliance. But an assessment of his presidency yields mixed results. His ability to stimulate the economy and to foster major tax reforms must be weighed against the astronomical increase in the federal deficit that occurred during his administration. His achievements in arms control and ending the Cold War are tempered, in the assessment of some historians, by the public embarrassment of the Iran-Contra scandal.

Reagan was born on February 6, 1911, in Tampico, Illinois. After graduating from Eureka College in 1932, he worked for a few years as sportscaster, then was put under contract with Warner Brothers, a major Hollywood studio. By 1947, he was one of the top actors in Hollywood, and he eventually appeared in fifty films, including *Bedtime for Bonzo* (1951).

In 1947, Reagan was elected to his first of six terms as president of the Screen Actors Guild (SAG). As SAG president, Reagan expelled what he believed were communists from the guild and made all other members swear an oath of loyalty to the United States. Originally a Democrat, Reagan switched to the Republican Party in 1962. Four years later, he ran for governor of California on a platform that called for the downsizing of the California state government. He won easily, and was reelected in 1970.

In 1976, Reagan made an unsuccessful bid for the Republican presidential nomination.

ensure that enough Soviet MIRVs would be stopped so that the United States could effectively strike back.

The debate over the cost, effectiveness, and need for SDI came to an end with the collapse of the Soviet Union in 1991. In 1993, the administration of President Bill Clinton (1946–) announced that SDI was ended. It was to be replaced by a Ballistic Missile Defense Program with a substantially reduced budget.

Four years later, he won not only the Republican nomination but the presidency. Within three months of his inauguration, Reagan was shot by would-be assassin John Hinckley Jr. as he left a Washington hotel after having delivered a speech. Contrary to news reports at the time, he nearly died.

During his first term, Reagan vigorously pursued an anticommunist foreign-policy agenda. He increased defense spending by $1.2 trillion. In March 1983, he proposed the Strategic Defense Initiative (SDI or "Star Wars"), which was intended to protect the United States against a Soviet strategic-missile attack. On domestic issues, Reagan tried to carry out his pro-business economic agenda with tax breaks that would create a new prosperity that would "trickle down" to the middle and working classes through new jobs and pay increases. The plan never worked, and the federal deficit continued to grow at an alarming rate.

During Reagan's second presidential term, relations between the Soviet Union and the United States improved dramatically as Reagan and Soviet Premier Mikhail Gorbachev successfully negotiated major arms-control agreements, which resulted in a decrease in defense spending.

In late 1986, the Iran-Contra scandal came to light. The sale of arms to Iran in order to raise funds for Nicaraguan contra (counterrevolutionary) rebels had been specifically outlawed by the U.S. Congress. Disregarding those laws, the Reagan administration went ahead with the secret operation. The resulting criminal prosecution of several administration officials and questions about his management style led to negative political fallout for Reagan. *Photo reproduced by permission of the Ronald Reagan Library.*

❖ "TRICKLE-DOWN" ECONOMICS AND THE RISE OF THE DEFICIT

When Ronald Reagan (1911–) ran for president in 1980, he wanted to change the nation's economic path. He rejected the prevailing economic theory that had dominated American economic policy since World War II (1939–45). That theory held that the federal government should influence the actions of the business world with its policies. It also called for deficit

Vietnam Veterans Memorial

On November 13, 1982, 150,000 Vietnam veterans and their families gathered in Washington, D.C., for the dedication of the Vietnam Veterans Memorial. Funded through private contributions, the plan for the memorial had been conceived and established by the Vietnam Veterans Memorial Fund (VVMF), a nonprofit organization incorporated by a group of Vietnam veterans. Like the war to which it bore testimony, the memorial was surrounded by controversy at each stage of planning and construction. Many suggested America was still trying to ignore or forget the conflict that had caused so much division in the country and then ended in defeat. Criticism was especially heated regarding the design that won the competition for the memorial, submitted by Maya Ying Lin, a twenty-one-year-old undergraduate architecture student at Yale University.

Lin designed a V-shaped black granite wall, each side stretching more than two hundred feet, with a gently sloping plot of ground in between, giving visitors the sensation of walking down into the earth. The highly polished,

spending by the federal government. Deficit spending is the gap between what the government spends and what it takes in as income (mostly but not exclusively from taxes). To make up the difference between spending and income, the federal government borrows money from the private sector or from other governments, sometimes in the form of bonds. Therefore, every year that the government runs a deficit it adds to the national debt, the total amount of money owed by the government because of borrowing.

Some economists believe that deficit spending can be good in that it will stimulate the economy, as was the case when spending on World War II ended the Great Depression, the period of severe economic decline that began in 1929. Others economists believe that long-term deficit spending makes it harder for people in the private sector to borrow money. When those people borrow money to buy a house or start a business, they end up competing with the government for the available capital.

Indeed, one of the favored targets for Reagan's wrath was deficit spending. In 1980, the deficit facing the federal government was nearly $80 billion. This led Reagan to proclaim that the federal budget was out of control and mirrorlike surface was carved with the names of the more than fifty-eight thousand Americans killed or missing in the conflict in Southeast Asia. The names of the men and women were listed in the order they were killed, rather than alphabetically.

While some veterans and many others liked Lin's spare and moving design and the sense of peace it created around itself, many veterans expressed dismay at the color and simplicity of the design. Some leading conservative journalists labeled it an "outrage." To satisfy those who criticized the memorial design, the VVMF commissioned sculptor Frederick Hart to create a realistic sculpture to add to the existing plan. In 1984, his larger-than-life-size statue of three rifle-carrying soldiers, one black and two white, was unveiled approximately 150 feet away from the memorial.

Situated on the National Mall near the Lincoln Memorial, the memorial, known simply as "The Wall," soon became one of the most visited sites in the nation's capitol, attracting more than five million visitors in its first two years.

government was the problem, not the solution. Reagan promised to balance the budget and to bring a new type of economics to Washington: supply-side economics. During the 1980 presidential primaries, Republican presidential hopeful George Bush (1924–) labeled Reagan's plan "voodoo economics," although after the election Bush upheld Reagan's economic policies both as Reagan's vice president and after his own election to the presidency in 1988.

At the heart of supply-side economics was Reagan's belief that increasing government spending in hopes of stimulating the economy was wasteful. Instead, Reagan argued, taxes should be cut and incentives created to encourage savings and investment, especially for the wealthy. Given such economic breaks, the wealthy would invest in American companies, stimulating the economy. This prosperity would then "trickle down" to the average American worker in the form of jobs and wage increases. Reagan firmly believed that lower tax rates, with lower government spending, would in fact balance the federal budget, not increase deficit spending. Reagan and his budget director, David Stockman, spoke of reducing federal spending by $67 billion.

Miami Race Riot

The first large-scale urban riot in the United States in more than a decade broke out in Miami on May 17, 1980, after four white police officers were found not guilty in the brutal beating death of an African American motorist. By the time the rioting ended three days later, eighteen people had been killed, four hundred had been injured, and property damage had exceeded $50 million.

Arthur McDuffie, thirty-three, was a former U.S. Marine and an insurance agent. On December 17, 1979, he was riding a motorcycle in the early morning hours when he drove through a red light in north Miami. His driver's license had been suspended because of a bounced check written to pay for another traffic offense. When Dade County Metro police pursued him for running the light, he attempted to escape and, according to police, ran more than twenty-five additional red lights at speeds up to one hundred miles-per-hour before being apprehended by a dozen Miami and Metro police. Initial police reports indicated that he had crashed and hit his head on the ground, then resisted arrest so that police had to use force to arrest him.

However, Reagan had also promised to restore America's military might after a losing effort in the Vietnam War (1954–75) and a failed attempt to rescue hostages held by Iran in 1980. Fulfilling this promise resulted in the largest increase in peacetime military spending in the history of the United States. In 1981, the U.S. Congress overwhelmingly passed the Kemp-Roth tax cuts to put Reagan's economic theory into practice. The following year, Congress cut the projected federal spending by $35.1 billion and approved a three-year, 25 percent reduction in personal and business income taxes. After these measures, the combined federal income taxes on earned income paid by the top 1 percent of the U.S. population dropped from 50 percent in 1981 to 37.5 percent in 1983. The tax cuts were combined with modest cuts in spending on social programs and a massive increase in military spending. Americans enjoyed both continued government spending and lower tax rates. According to Reagan's original plan, such policies would produce a balanced budget by 1984.

They did not. During Reagan's two terms as president, the federal deficit rose dramatically, from a low of $128 billion in 1982 to a high of $221 bil-

When McDuffie died from head injuries four days later, questions were quickly raised. After a four-day investigation, the local prosecutor filed charges against six Metro police officers on charges ranging from participating in a cover-up to second-degree murder. Eventually, four officers went on trial. Because of the high emotions surrounding the case, the trial was moved to Tampa. The defense was successful in obtaining a jury of six white males. After hearing conflicting versions of who had done what from officers, some of whom received immunity from prosecution in exchange for their testimony, the jury acquitted the four men.

Following what many thought was an unjust verdict, especially since several officers had testified that McDuffie had been beaten as he lay hand-cuffed and defenseless on the ground, rioting broke out. The Justice Building in Miami was broken into and vandalized; dozens of cars were overturned or burned; and many people, mainly white, were pulled from their cars and beaten or killed. Order was restored only after Florida's governor called out thirty-six hundred National Guardsmen, bringing to an end the worst race riot in American history up to that time.

lion in 1986. The accumulated debt of the six years of deficit spending, from 1981 to 1987, was more than $1.1 trillion. When Reagan left office in 1988, the national debt was $2.6 trillion, compared with the $914 billion debt he inherited from the administration of President Jimmy Carter (1924–). In 1986, the United States became a debtor nation, the largest in the world.

❖ THE IRAN-CONTRA SCANDAL

In the fall of 1986, two seemingly separate and secret arms deals were revealed to the nation. During the next few years, the American public became transfixed by even more revelations that would become known as the Iran-Contra scandal. In a series of highly publicized hearings, special investigations, and prosecutions of high-ranking officials in the administration of President Ronald Reagan (1911–), it was revealed that a secret government operating within the official one had charge of U.S. foreign policy. The Iran-Contra scandal threatened to result in impeachment proceedings against the president of the United States and to cause the utter collapse of public confidence in the integrity of government.

A joint congressional investigation and a specially appointed prosecutor probed the allegations that lawbreaking reached into the highest offices in the land. In the end, however, the U.S. Congress decided that only a handful of junior officials in the Reagan administration had broken the law. While the president himself was negligent in the supervision of his appointees, neither he nor Vice President George Bush (1924–) were found guilty of any crimes personally. In all, fourteen men were prosecuted for various charges, and none were penalized with anything more than fines. While several minor players received light sentences, most of these were overturned on appeal on the grounds that the men had been granted immunity (freedom from penalty) to testify before Congress and thus could not be incriminated or found guilty by any statements they made in the Iran-Contra hearings, despite admitting to breaking the law.

The scandal began on October 5, 1986, when a plane piloted by an agent of the Central Intelligence Agency (CIA) was shot down over Nicaragua. The plane's cargo bay was full of weapons intended for Nicaraguan rebels, known as contras (counterrevolutionaries), for use against Nicaragua's communist government. Since Congress had passed laws in 1982 and 1984 expressly forbidding attempts both to overthrow the government of Nicaragua and to arm the contras, the captured weapons revealed evidence that the Reagan administration had broken the law. Initially Reagan said his administration had no connection to this flight, but subsequent revelations proved this to be false.

Less than five weeks later, a Lebanese newspaper revealed that Robert McFarlane, Reagan's special assistant for national security, had engaged in secret arms-for-hostages deals with the Iranian government of the Ayatollah Ruhollah Khomeini (1900–1989). During the early 1980s, Western hostages were seized and held by pro-Iranian terrorists throughout the Middle East. After the ordeal of fifty-two American hostages taken by Iran in 1979 and held for more than a year, the U.S. government officially decided never to make such trades with terrorist governments. The most shocking revelation, however, was that money obtained by secretly selling arms to Iran was being channeled back to the contras to arm them. The Reagan administration claimed that by selling arms to Iran, it was trying to win the favor of more-reasonable politicians in that nation's government and to win release of hostages. The administration also stated that the money paid for the arms was controlled by a single National Security Council (NSC) staffer: U.S. Marine Lieutenant Colonel Oliver North.

Holes in the official story soon surfaced. On November 6, 1986, Reagan had said that reports about arms sales had "no foundation." On

November 13, he admitted the sales, but denied they were for hostages. Six days later, he declared that such sales were, in fact, legal. Under controversial powers granted by the National Security Act, the president is sometimes able to bypass the law (legally) by issuing what is called a "finding," in which national security issues are claimed to override any legal checks. U.S. Attorney General Edwin Meese said that Reagan had signed such a finding in order to override the acts passed by Congress. It was revealed late that Reagan did so only after the fact. Moreover, Reagan failed to inform Congress of this finding in a timely manner as the law specified and did so only when the scandal broke.

Several investigations were mounted in the wake of the Iran-Contra revelations. The first was the Tower Commission, named after its chair, former Republican Senator John Tower of Texas. Appointed by Reagan to conduct a review of the NSC's role, the Tower Commission issued its report on February 26, 1987, blaming the NSC's staff and concluding the affair was the result of Reagan's notoriously poor management skills. The American public, however, demanded a better accounting, and Congress took the unprecedented step of conducting publicly televised hearings in the summer of 1987.

North testified that he had altered official NSC documents to cover for the president. U.S. Navy Admiral John Poindexter, North's supervisor, also revealed he had destroyed documents so the president would not be politically embarrassed. North later admitted to shredding thousands of documents that would have proven his guilt, and presumably many others, up to and including Reagan. Testifying under congressional immunity, North, McFarlane, and Poindexter admitted some of their illegal activities. North, understanding that he was being made a scapegoat, claimed that he believed Reagan knew and approved of his actions. Poindexter, however, denied this. North went so far as to insist that William Casey, director of the Central Intelligence Agency, had personally approved his secret operations, but since Casey died during this period, he could not be questioned personally.

The most important and far-reaching investigation was carried out by Special Prosecutor Lawrence E. Walsh. At first, the Reagan administration tried to avoid sponsoring an independent investigation, but soon realized this might appear an obstruction of justice. From the beginning, Walsh, a noted former government prosecutor, immediately showed his intent to be independent and thorough. Fighting an uphill battle, in many cases against former friends who labeled him a turncoat, Walsh doggedly pursued as many leads as possible. His final report concluded that the policies at the heart of the Iran-Contra scandal matter were developed at the

Mikhail Gorbachev

The Communist Party ran the government of the Union of Soviet Socialist Republics, more commonly known as the Soviet Union, for almost seventy years. When Mikhail Gorbachev became leader of the Soviet Communist Party in the mid-1980s, he introduced economic and social reforms that radically transformed the lives of the Soviet people and had a profound effect on nations around the world. He helped improved relations between the Soviet Union and the United States and reduced the threat of global nuclear war. In the process, he brought an end to his own leadership and to the Soviet Union.

Gorbachev was born on March 2, 1931, to peasant farmers in the tiny farm village of Privolnoe near the Caucasus Mountains in the southwestern region of the Soviet Union. In 1950, he entered Moscow State University to study law. While in school, he met and married Raisa Maksimovna Titorenko. He also joined the Communist Party, and after graduating in 1955, he began to work for the Party.

Over the next three decades, Gorbachev rose steadily through the leadership ranks of the Communist Party. In 1985, after a series of deaths of the Party's top leaders, Gorbachev was appointed general secretary (leader) of the Communist Party, making him the effective leader of his country.

Gorbachev immediately began a campaign of reforms in the Soviet Union. He forced many conservative Communist leaders out of government and replaced them with younger members who shared his views. He began policies called *perestroika* (restructuring) and *glasnost* (openness) that

"highest levels" of the Reagan administration. Every senior cabinet member involved in foreign policy had knowledge of the affair, and many of them lied to cover up their and the president's knowledge. Walsh's report also points out that following the initial Iran-Contra revelations, these officials "deliberately deceived the Congress and the public" about their support for illegal operations.

Walsh charged fourteen individuals with criminal violations. North and Poindexter were tried and found guilty of various charges, but their convictions were overturned on appeal because they had been granted removed government controls over the economy and allowed the Soviet people to openly discuss the problems facing their country.

Gorbachev also sought peace abroad and at home. After a series of summit conferences, he and U.S. president Ronald Reagan signed a treaty in 1987 limiting the number of nuclear weapons each country could have. In 1989, Gorbachev ended the Afghanistan War, which had pitted anticommunist Afghans against their government and the Soviet Union since 1978. For all of his peace efforts, Gorbachev was awarded the Nobel Peace Prize in 1990.

The end of the Soviet Union began in 1989 when Gorbachev allowed other political parties to run against the Communists in general elections. The Communists lost their power and Gorbachev separated himself from them by taking the position of Soviet president. As communism weakened across Eastern Europe, many countries and ethnic groups wanted their independence. Gorbachev sought to maintain control, but his people wanted freedom and reforms quicker than he was willing to give it to them.

In August 1991, after a failed coup (overthrow of the government) by Communist leaders, Gorbachev dissolved the Communist Party. He then granted independence to the remaining Soviet-controlled republics. On December 8, 1991, a new economic federation, the Commonwealth of Independent States, was formed among those republics. On Christmas Day, Gorbachev resigned the office of president, becoming a private citizen. At midnight on December 31, 1991, the Union of Soviet Socialist Republics ceased to exist.

immunity by Congress. McFarlane pleaded guilty to withholding information and to lying before Congress, but he received a short sentence. As Walsh said in his final report:

> The underlying facts of Iran/contra are that, regardless of criminality, President Reagan, the secretary of state, the secretary of defense, and the director of central intelligence and their necessary assistants committed themselves, however reluctantly, to two programs contrary to congressional policy and contrary to national policy. They skirted the law, some of them broke the law, and almost all of them tried to cover up the President's willful activities.

❖ END OF THE COLD WAR

The cold war was not a time of war in the traditional sense, but it was a period of extreme political tension that arose after World War II (1939–45) between the United States and its allies and the Soviet Union and its allies. Many people believed President Ronald Reagan (1911–) finally brought an end to the cold war by building up the American military and doggedly pursuing an anticommunist foreign policy during his terms in office. While these measures may have helped end the cold war, they did not do so alone. The actions of Reagan's counterpart, Soviet Premier Mikhail Gorbachev (1931–) helped as much, if not more so.

The early 1980s saw rapid changes in the leadership of the Soviet Union. Leonid Brezhnev (1906–1982), who had led the Soviet Union since 1964, died in 1982 and was succeeded by Yuri Andropov (1914–1984). When Andropov died two years later, he was succeeded by Konstantin Chernenko (1911–1985). Less than a year later, Chernenko died and fifty-four-year-old Mikhail Gorbachev became the new Soviet premier. Gorbachev ushered in a new era of Soviet leadership: He and many of his generation of leaders were better educated and more widely traveled than their predecessors.

Almost immediately, Gorbachev unleashed revolutionary reforms in Soviet politics and economics. He instituted a policy of *glasnost* ("openness") in Soviet society, increasing freedom of speech and assembly and introducing new rights for consumers, employees, and managers. His *perestroika* ("restructuring") policy provided greater incentives and rewards for workers and managers, modernized technology, and opened the Soviet Union to world trade and foreign investment. In foreign policy, Gorbachev wanted friendlier relations with the United States, to see further reductions in conventional and strategic weapons, and to downscale or eliminate Soviet influence in Third World conflicts.

Gorbachev was motivated in part by the notion that money saved from a reduction of military spending for costly efforts abroad could stimulate the Soviet domestic economy, which was hurting. Politically, he could justify such cuts only by persuading the United States to agree to similar cuts in strategic and conventional forces and by resolving some of the ongoing conflicts in the Third World.

Although tensions between the United States and the Soviet Union were still high in 1985, Reagan and Gorbachev decided to meet in Geneva, Switzerland, in November of that year. While no major agreements were reached, each leader came away from the meeting believing he could work with the other. Three sets of arms-control talks continued in Geneva: talks on reducing or eliminating intermediate-range missiles, on reducing strategic arms, and on issues related to space and defense.

The Reagan administration was deeply suspicious of Gorbachev's pronounced willingness to lessen tensions between the two superpowers. Many in the administration considered it a ploy to undermine the relationship between the United States and its European allies. Despite protests from the Soviets, Reagan continued to develop his plan for the Strategic Defense Initiative (SDI), a space-based military system that would shield the United States against a possible nuclear-missile attack by the Soviet Union.

The dismantling of the Berlin Wall. **Reproduced by permission of the Corbis Corporation.**

In September 1986, Gorbachev proposed to Reagan that the two leaders meet in Reykjavík, Iceland, on October 11 and 12. Gorbachev seemed to suggest that he was willing to reach an agreement on intermediate missiles without needing an agreement that would place limits on SDI. When the two leaders met, Gorbachev stunned everyone by first proposing that each side reduce it strategic missiles by 50 percent. The following day, he further shocked the world by proposing that the two countries eliminate all nuclear weapons over a period of ten years. The talks stalled, however, because the two sides could not come to an agreement over SDI.

Finally, in a summit in Washington, D.C., on December 8, 1987, Reagan and Gorbachev signed the Intermediate Nuclear Forces (INF) Treaty. Under the terms of the treaty, both sides agreed to withdraw and destroy all intermediate-range nuclear weapons from their arsenals (the treaty was ratified by the U.S. Congress in May 1988).

In 1988, Gorbachev began reducing Soviet presence in countries in Europe and in other parts of the world. In February, he announced the Soviet Union would begin to withdraw from Afghanistan where it had fought a war with the Afghanistan government against Afghan rebels since 1979. (The withdrawal was completed one year later.) In December, in a speech before the United Nations, Gorbachev announced the Soviet Union would withdraw five hundred thousand troops and ten thousand tanks from Eastern Europe.

These troops had ensured the stability of pro-Soviet communist governments in the region. Without them, these governments began to collapse. The governments in Poland, Hungary, Czechoslovakia, Bulgaria, and Romania all fell quickly. On November 10, 1989, the Berlin Wall separating East Germany and West Germany was torn down. The following year, the two countries were reunited.

As communists lost control across Europe, so, too, did the Soviet Union lose control over its empire. Citizens in countries that were part of the Soviet Union began to assert their independence and freedom. At the end of 1991, powerless in the face of rising protests, the Soviet Union was dissolved, bringing an end to the cold war.

✤ For More Information

BOOKS

Huber, Peter William. *Sandra Day O'Connor.* Minneapolis, MN: Econo-Clad Books, 1999.

Johnson, Darv. *The Reagan Years.* San Diego, CA: Lucent Books, 2000.

Lawson, Don, and Barbara Silberdick Feinberg. *America Held Hostage: The Iran Hostage Crisis and the Iran-Contra Affair.* New York: Franklin Watts, 1991.

Noonan, Peggy. *When Character Was King: A Story of Ronald Reagan.* New York: Viking, 2001.

Porter, Bruce D., and Marvin Dunn. *The Miami Riot of 1980: Crossing the Bounds.* Lanham, MD: Lexington Books, 1984.

Slansky, Paul. *The Clothes Have No Emperor: A Chronicle of the American '80s.* New York: Fireside Books, 1989.

WEB SITES

The Cold War. http://library.thinkquest.org/22059/index2.html (accessed on July 29, 2002).

Dave Leip's Atlas of U.S. Presidential Elections. http://www.uselectionatlas.org/USPRESIDENT/frametextj.html (accessed on July 29, 2002).

Ronald Reagan Presidential Foundation and Library. http://www.reaganfoundation. org/ (accessed on July 29, 2002).

The Strategic Defense Initiative (SDI). http://www.school-for-champions.com/ history/sdi.htm (accessed on July 29, 2002).

The Vietnam Veterans Memorial Wall Page. http://thewall-usa.com/ (accessed on July 29, 2002).

Walsh Iran/Contra Report. http://www.fas.org/irp/offdocs/walsh/ (accessed on July 29, 2002).

chapter five *Lifestyles and Social Trends*

1980: Marilyn Ferguson's *The Aquarian Conspiracy,* explaining the philosophy and ideas of the New Age movement, is published.

1980: *The Official Preppy Handbook,* edited by Lisa Birnbach, is published.

1980: June 1 Atlanta entrepreneur Ted Turner debuts the twenty-four-hour news channel Cable Network News (CNN).

1981: January 20 Ronald Reagan is inaugurated as president; his wife, Nancy, wears a white inaugural-ball gown designed by James Galanos; her complete inaugural wardrobe reportedly costs $25,000.

1981: September 1 A study released by the Equal Employment Opportunity Commission finds that women's earnings remain at about 60 percent of men's earnings in comparable jobs.

1982: Reebok athletic shoes, introduced in fashion colors, overtake Nike running shoes in sales.

1982: Rubik's Cube, a puzzle for which the solution proves frustrating and even obsessive for many, sells wildly in the United States and in other countries.

1982: May 7 Baptist evangelist Billy Graham leads more than 600 religious leaders in a weeklong antinuclear conference held in the Soviet Union.

1982: June 30 The Equal Right Amendment (ERA) misses the deadline for ratification after it fails to get the support of the full thirty-eight states necessary.

1983: First Lady Nancy Reagan begins a nationwide program to combat drug abuse and uses the slogan "Just Say No."

1983: November 20 Approximately 100 million people view *The Day After,* a controversial ABC movie simulating the effects of a nuclear war on a Kansas town.

1984: April 16 A two-year study of religious television reports that more than 13 million Americans watch religious television programming on a regular basis.

1984: May 1 A report by the U.S. Department of Housing and Urban Development estimates the nation's homeless population as numbering between 250,000 and 350,000. Many other national organizations claim there are actually ten times that many homeless Americans.

1984: July 23 Vanessa Williams becomes the first Miss America to resign in the history of the pageant when a men's magazine announces it will publish nude photographs of her.

1984: September 16 The television series *Miami Vice* debuts on NBC. It soon influences men's styles: sports coats worn over T-shirts, both in pastel colors.

1985: Street style, the deliberately under-dressed look of youth, is the height of fashion.

1985: Crack, crystallized cocaine that can be smoked to produce a short but intense high, is introduced into the United States.

1986: May 25 More than 5 million people form a human chain from New York City to Long Beach, California, in Hands Across America, a project organized to call attention to poverty, hunger, and homelessness in the country.

1986: July 10 The National Institute on Drug Abuse reports that the number of Americans killed each year in cocaine-related deaths rose from 185 in 1981 to more than 560 in 1985.

1987: March 3 Many well-known actors and politicians take part in the "Grate American Sleep-Out" to draw attention to the plight of the homeless in America.

1987: March 19 Praise the Lord (PTL) founder Jim Bakker resigns after revelations that he committed adultery and stole funds from his ministry.

1988: February 21 Before 6,000 of his followers, televangelist Jimmy Swaggart tearfully confesses to an unspecified sin. Later, his ministry is taken away when it is revealed that he had sexual relations with a prostitute.

1988: May 15 Televangelist Marion "Pat" Robertson files papers to create a new political action committee, Americans for the Republic, that will train and fund conservative Christian political candidates.

1989: March 24 Disbarred lawyer Joel B. Steinberg is given the maximum prison sentence of eight to twenty-years for the beating death of his six-year-old adopted daughter.

1989: June 10 The Moral Majority is officially disbanded.

✳ *Overview*

In the 1980s, American culture was defined by a proud political and social conservatism. The election of Republican Ronald Reagan to the presidency in 1980 was the high-water mark of late twentieth-century American conservatism. (Conservatives, represented by the Republican Party, favor preserving traditional values and customs. They oppose any sudden change to the arrangement of power in the country, and they believe the federal government should have limited control over the lives of American citizens. On the other hand, liberals, represented by the Democratic Party, favor a stronger central government. They believe in political reforms that extend democracy, distribute wealth more evenly, and bring about social change.)

During his two terms as chief executive, Reagan tried to abolish the so-called welfare state and reduce the size of the federal government. Reagan and his administration believed that eliminating federal bureaucracy and regulations would allow American business to return to doing what it did best: producing a mountain of goods for a mass-consumption society.

The Reagan presidency brought high style back to the White House, and Americans wanted to copy that style and elegance. Urged on by their president to spend, Americans did so. American culture became a culture of consumption as shopping became Americans' number-one hobby. For some, shopping became a religion and the shopping mall the new American church.

A good education, a good job, and a loving family no longer defined success for many Americans. They had to have an M.B.A. degree, a high-paying job, an elegant home or apartment, a membership to an upscale health club, and the necessary clothes to give at least the appearance they had succeeded. Indeed, for these Americans, called "yuppies," dressing for success became the rule to live by. They wanted more, and they were in a hurry to get it. Popular phrases that arose in the decade—"A.S.A.P." (as soon as possible), "what's the bottom line?," and "cut to the chase"—communicated their sense of urgency as they sought money and a way of life that flaunted it.

Beyond the shopping malls and mail-order catalogs, serious social issues made news, and some people were concerned. While many Americans spent freely, others were left with nothing as the Reagan administration stopped providing financial support for numerous social programs. As increasing numbers of Americans lost their homes, they found society had neither the means nor the will to help them in their time of crisis. Many of them were left to wander the streets of American cities, swelling the ranks of the homeless. Reports of child abuse also soared during the decade, overwhelming social service agencies. Officials finally declared the problem of child abuse "a national emergency." As with homelessness, American society's attempts to address child abuse were often inadequate.

The substantial fear of a nuclear war also weighed heavy on the minds of many Americans in the 1980s. President Reagan was staunchly anti-communist, and he created a nuclear arms race with the Soviet Union that led many to believe a nuclear war was not only possible but inevitable. Americans from all levels of society people banded together in a movement to stop the arms race, but their protests went unheard in the White House. Only a change in Soviet leadership led to reduced tensions between the two major nuclear powers of the world and allowed Americans some relief from their fear of nuclear war.

In this decade of excess, Americans still found time for religion. Many polls showed that the majority of people in the country had a strong belief in a Supreme Being and an afterlife. Yet many found it difficult to adhere to the strict traditions of their churches, and they sought out other forms of religions. The New Age movement, a blend of eastern philosophies and centuries-old mystical beliefs, captured the attention of millions of Americans. The polar opposite of New Agers were televangelists or television evangelists. They saw their audiences grow dramatically, and they became rich in the process. Armed with money and the ears of many Americans, these evangelists tried to use their pulpits to convert people to their religious and political beliefs. Some even went so far as to enter national politics.

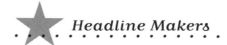

Christie Brinkley (1953–) Supermodel Christie Brinkley embodied not only the all-American look of the 1980s but also the fantasy life of many women in the decade. According to many, Brinkley had it all: a successful career, a marriage to pop musician Billy Joel, and a healthy child. By the end of the decade, Brinkley's wide smile and blue eyes had appeared on more than two hundred magazine covers. Her classic good looks appealed to many men while her successful ability to juggle family and career appealed to many women across the country. *Photo reproduced by permission of Archive Photos, Inc.*

Terry Cole-Whittaker (1939–) Terry Cole-Whittaker was a popular minister in the early 1980s. Based in San Diego, "Reverend Terry," as she was known to her followers, broadcast her message each Sunday on a syndicated television program that reached millions. Stressing that "You can have it all—now!," she encouraged her listeners week after week to seek prosperity, power, and abundance. Blending New Age spirituality, science of mind, and pop and motivational psychology, Cole-Whittaker provided her followers with newsletters and instructional tapes. In 1985, for reasons not entirely clear, she ended her ministry.

Bill Cosby (1937–) Actor and comedian Bill Cosby became one of the most popular television personalities of the 1980s with the success of *The Cosby Show*. The situation comedy portrayed an intelligent, affluent, nonstereotypical African American family as no television show had done before. For Cosby, the show was a response to the increasingly violent shows television offered. Although *The Cosby Show* received some criticism for ignoring issues facing the African American community, the show earned some of the highest ratings on television from its debut in the 1984 season. *Photo reproduced by permission of AP/Wide World Photos.*

Jerry Falwell (1933–) Jerry Falwell was largely responsible for the union of fundamentalist religion and national politics in the 1980s. A fundamentalist preacher, Falwell was the founder and spokesman for the conservative religious organization known as the Moral Majority. With chapters in all fifty states, the Moral Majority tried to increase the presence of religion in all aspects of American life, cultural as well as political. The success of the organization, however, was limited, as the majority of Americans decided, as voters, that they did not want matters of public policy to be decided by religious leaders. *Photo reproduced by permission of the Corbis Corporation.*

Shelby Steele (1946–) Shelby Steele, a professor of English at San Jose State University in California, became an outspoken opponent of racial preferences and affirmative action in the late 1980s. In magazine articles and in many interviews, Steele downplayed the significance of racism. He insisted that African Americans needed to return to a sense of self-reliance promoted by the civil rights movement of the 1960s. Black leaders and liberals often dismissed his views, implying he had sold out to those who did not have the best interest of blacks at heart. *Photo reproduced by permission of Ed Kashi/TIME Magazine.*

Martha Stewart (1941–) Martha Stewart emerged during the 1980s as America's foremost authority on entertaining and decorating, catering to the country's growing taste for the good life. In her books and television appearances, Stewart created impossibly perfect desserts and decorations, often from everyday materials. She made it seem as though anyone could do the same, and many believed her. By the mid-1980s, her company was making $1 million a year. In 1987, Stewart entered into a business relationship with K-Mart, which began marketing her products such as linens and dishes. *Photo reproduced by permission of the Corbis Corporation.*

Ted Turner (1938–) Ted Turner became one of the pioneers of the blossoming cable-television industry in the 1980s. At the end of the previous decade, Turner's innovative superstation WTBS was one of the best-known cable networks in America, reaching three million viewers in addition to cable subscribers in six southern states. In June 1980, he launched Cable News Network (CNN), a twenty-four-hour, all-news channel. It soon transformed broadcast journalism. By 1989, four networks of the Turner Broadcasting System—WTBS, CNN, CNN Headline News, TNT—were in millions of homes in the United States and abroad. Turner had become a billionaire. *Photo reproduced by permission of the Corbis Corporation.*

Vanessa Williams (1963–) Vanessa Williams made headlines in the 1980s for two "firsts" in American history: She was the first African American to be crowned Miss America and the first Miss America to resign her crown. Miss America officials forced Williams to resign the crown two months before her year-long reign ended in 1984 because of the publication in a men's magazine of nude photographs taken of Williams when she was nineteen. The public sympathized with Williams, and she emerged in the late 1980s as a successful pop singer and actress in television shows and theater productions. *Photo reproduced by permission of the Corbis Corporation.*

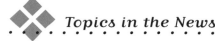

❖ CONSUMERISM: THE NEW GREAT AMERICAN PASTIME

In 1981, President Ronald Reagan (1911–) set the tone for an increase in spending by American consumers by celebrating his inauguration with eleven million dollars' worth of pageantry and balls. It was a signal to the nation that glitter was back in style. First Lady Nancy Reagan soon oversaw expensive renovations at the White House and ordered a new set of White House china that cost more than two hundred thousand dollars. Although none of these expensive projects was financed with public funds, the Reagans were criticized for an extravagance that seemed inappropriate during the economic recession (short period of economic decline) that plagued the early 1980s. Yet the "small is beautiful" philosophy that had charmed some in the 1970s was put aside for good in the decade that followed.

All across the United States there was a huge assortment of goods and services to buy. As the president reminded Americans, the only limits they had were those they imposed on themselves. "We are living in a material world, and I am a material girl," Madonna sang in her 1985 hit "Material Girl." The song served not only as her theme song that decade, but as one for American shoppers, as well. With thousands of malls, supermarkets, and restaurants to visit, everything necessary for the good life appeared to be for sale. And Americans bought.

Various observers began to assert that shopping had become Americans' favorite leisure activity. During a five-year period at mid-decade, the 91 million U.S. households purchased 62 million microwave ovens, 63 million VCRs, 57 million washers and dryers, 88 million cars and light trucks, 105 million color television sets, 31 million cordless phones, and 30 million telephone answering machines. It was the greatest spending spree in America since the boom that followed World War II (1939–45). Surveys showed that Americans were spending more time in malls than anywhere else except home, job, or school. They made seven billion trips in and out of shopping centers every year. By 1985, there were more than twenty-six thousand shopping centers in the country, with total annual purchases at those centers reaching $1 trillion.

The shopping mall was challenged by one unexpected competitor: home shopping. In a trend that began in the 1960s and increased in the 1980s, businesses both large and small moved into American homes via mail-order catalogs. Department stores, art museums, various nonprofit charitable groups, and new mail-order outlets began competing with old-time mail-order companies such as Sears, Montgomery Ward, and L. L.

Rubik's Cube

Perhaps the most popular toy sold in the United States in the early 1980s was Rubik's Cube. Invented in the 1970s by Ernö Rubik, a Hungarian professor of design, Rubik's Cube was the most challenging (and for many people, infuriating) puzzle ever to achieve mass-market success. The six-sided cube was composed of twenty-six smaller cubes or "cubies." Nine cubies, separated into three horizontal and three vertical rows, made up a side. When the cube was purchased, each of the nine cubies on a side was of a uniform color, different from those on the other sides. After the horizontal and vertical rows were rotated randomly, the cube would end up a jumble of colors. The point was to restore the cube to its original state, with all the colors uniform on each side. Most people had no idea how to do it. Some spent hours, if not days, rearranging the cube in dozens of the more than forty-three quintillion possible positions other than the one correct position before achieving success or giving up altogether.

The puzzle could be solved, of course, as Rubik and many others demonstrated. People who had figured out a system for solving the puzzle wrote best-selling books on how to do it. Contests with lubricated cubes were held around the world to see who could solve it in the fastest time. In 1982, in a world championship contest in Budapest, Hungary, a high-school student from Los Angeles solved the puzzle in 22.95 seconds.

With international sales of the cube in the millions, Rubik soon became the richest person in Hungary.

Bean. Another complement to home shopping was the emerging phenomenon of television channels such as Home Shopping Network and QVC Network. The home-shopping industry grew from sales of $1 million in 1982 to sales of $1.4 billion by 1989. Home shopping was made especially easy by credit cards. By the mid-1980s, the average credit card holder carried seven cards; the number of Mastercard and Visa charge cards held by American consumers was estimated to be 125 million. Credit cards were directly responsible for an explosion in consumer debt during the decade.

❖ THE RISE OF THE "YUPPIES" AND DRESSING FOR SUCCESS

Inspired by a victory in World War II (1939–45) and increasing economic prosperity, America experienced a boom in the birth of babies follow-

Feminism Flounders

The women's liberation movement (also referred to as feminism or the women's rights movement) in the 1970s had been marked by two triumphs: The 1973 Supreme Court decision in *Roe* v. *Wade,* which protected a woman's right to choose an abortion, and the congressional approval of the Equal Rights Amendment (ERA) in 1972. Both these victories came under heated attack in the 1980s. A decisive sign of the power of the backlash against the women's movement was the defeat of the ERA in 1982.

The ERA, which stated that "equality of rights under the law shall not be denied or abridged by the United States or by any State on account of sex," needed the approval of three-fourths of the states before it could become an amendment to the U.S. Constitution. The deadline for approval or ratification was June 1982. Its supporters argued there were many forms of discrimination against women, which could be stopped only by an explicit constitutional guarantee of women's equality. Public-opinion polls showed that the majority of women and men favored the measure, and by

ing the war. The millions of Americans born between the years 1946 and 1964 have been labeled by the media and others as baby boomers. When they came of age in the 1960s and 1970s, they were faced with an unpopular war in Vietnam, rising social unrest, rights movements by minorities and women, governmental scandals, energy crises, and a poor economy.

As the recession (short period of economic decline) of the early 1980s gave way to economic prosperity in America, many baby boomers responded enthusiastically to the call of President Ronald Reagan (1911–) to invest in the American economy. A concern for social justice was soon replaced by a need for success in the minds of many baby boomers. Very materialistic, they focused on careers and the good life promised by the American Dream. By mid-decade, these young, educated, city-dwelling baby boomers were called "yuppies" (young urban professionals), and the name stuck.

Defined by one research group as people between the ages of twenty-five and thirty-nine, with incomes of at least forty thousand dollars from a professional or management job, yuppies were estimated to total four mil-

1977, thirty-five of the thirty-eight states required for its ratification had already given their approval.

Yet by the late 1970s, the ERA campaign had lost momentum, and partly because a determined opposition had arisen. Opponents of the amendment argued that women's rights were already protected by laws. Passing the ERA, they asserted, would give far too much power to the federal government. In addition, it would further serve to blur gender roles already challenged by the feminist movement. In the end, despite broad public support, the ERA failed to gain approval in the three final state legislatures necessary for its ratification.

The defeat of the ERA, the rising influence of antiabortion groups, and a growing criticism of feminism in general soon led many to believe that the women's liberation movement was on the decline. Despite this, polls at the end of the decade showed a large majority of Americans still supported the principles of equal rights for women and of a woman's right to choose abortion. At the same time, most women also believed that feminism had significantly improved their lives.

lion in 1984. By less restrictive definitions, estimates of the number of yuppies in the United States reached twenty million. Whatever their number, they became highly visible and much discussed. Many considered them to be the trendsetters of their generation. Celebrating their increasingly high profile in American life, *Newsweek* magazine dubbed 1984 "The Year of the Yuppie."

During the 1980s, many yuppies enrolled in business schools and pursued an M.B.A. (master's of business administration). Declared the yuppie degree, the M.B.A. was seen as a passport to high pay and rapid advancement in corporate America. Enrollment in business schools increased dramatically in each year in the decade. In 1984 alone, an estimated two hundred thousand students were pursuing an M.B.A. At least one-third of those were women.

Not all yuppies earned M.B.A. degrees, but they did tend to share a fairly identifiable lifestyle. Most yuppies lived and worked in metropolitan areas, the centers for the high-paying jobs they usually sought. They seemed to be hard-driving overachievers who thought little of working late at the office, bringing work home, and working weekends if necessary. Yuppies placed a high importance on appearance. Living by the motto "dress for success," men were frequently seen wearing business suits from upscale stores such as Brooks Brothers, carrying shiny leather briefcases, and checking the Rolex watches on their wrists. Women wore conservative navy or black blazers, knee-covering skirts, unadorned white blouses closed at the neck with a tied bow, and conservative low heels.

For more-relaxed occasions and on weekends, yuppie men and women wore trendy and fashionable Nike and Adidas running shoes and bought clothing from stores such as Banana Republic or catalogues such as L. L. Bean. They tended to dress as though they were off on a great outdoor adventure even while just running errands around the city.

❖ THE HEALTH CLUB CRAZE AND FITNESS STYLE

A healthy escape from the demands of a busy professional life, exercise became the new pastime for both men and women in the 1980s. Yuppies in particular were health conscious. Some jogged, continuing the trend from the 1970s, while many others joined health spas or clubs. Capitalizing on the yuppies' interest in their physical appearance, the upscale health clubs offered high-tech, computerized equipment and all the latest exercise machinery. In addition, they offered personal trainers, aerobics classes, racquetball courts, squash courts, swimming pools, steam rooms, saunas, and masseurs and masseuses. Many featured fresh juice bars as well, satisfying the yuppies' desire for natural foods and nutrition. Since many clubs were coed, the management often played up the social possibilities of membership. Indeed, for many yuppies, health clubs seemed nearly to replace singles' bars as prime places to meet members of the opposite sex.

Trying to prove their competence in the professional world, women transferred this sense of competition into improving their appearance. They became immersed in body improvements that began with aerobic dance classes and sometimes led to surgical changes such as cellulite removal, tummy tucks, and face peels. Clothes of the decade were greatly influenced by this obsession. The exercise gear that women (and men) wore to aerobics classes was soon seen on the street as well. The new fabrics were comfortable, breathable knits: cotton fleece and shimmering spandex that hugged the skin, showing off newly formed arm muscles and lean legs. The fabrics were used in everything from stirrup pants, leggings, tights, tank tops, midriff-baring tops, bicycle shorts, and jogging suits. One-piece bodysuits or other body-hugging items were layered with loose sweatshirts or T-shirts ripped to reveal a shoulder, as seen in the 1983 movie *Flashdance*.

❖ FROM THE PREPPY LOOK TO STREET FASHION

While many women in the 1980s opted for an athletic look on weekends, many men dressed in what was called a "preppy" style. Like their weekday business attire, this style of clothes reflected the conservative values and the importance of appearing to be wealthy that many sought in the decade. With classically styled jeans, khakis, or long shorts, men sported the typical preppy shirt: the polo shirt (also called a tennis shirt) with a three-button placket, ribbed collar, and a small logo (polo player, alligator, or royal crest) on the left breast. The ever-present logo, which altered depending on the brand of shirt, became one of the many status symbols of Americans. People were so concerned with emblems of their financial success that a plain shirt was often difficult to find.

The preppy style recalled the clothes traditionally worn by students in Eastern collegiate or preparatory schools (hence the name preppy): tan khakis; rugby shirts; turtlenecks; white, pink, or pale blue button-down oxford shirts; navy blue blazers; and penny loafers, often worn without socks as *The Official Preppy Handbook* (1980) suggested. The look also included the popular tennis sweater (a white V-neck with blue-

Gyms and health clubs became trendy during the 1980s. Reproduced by permission of the Corbis Corporation.

The Cocaine Crisis

In the 1980s, few subjects were in the news as much as cocaine. There were two main stages to the growing problem of cocaine use in the United States. During the early part of the decade, many people considered cocaine a harmless, even glamorous, "recreational" drug that was nonaddictive. It was the drug of choice of the famous and successful: professional athletes, celebrities in the arts and entertainment, lawyers, university professors, and Wall Street brokers. They were among the few who could afford the high-priced drug. Sometimes called the "champagne of drugs," the white powder became a status symbol at yuppie parties.

By 1985, twelve million people in the United States were estimated to be frequent cocaine users. Statistics began to appear that showed an increase in cocaine-related crimes. Drug gangs, which controlled the trafficking of cocaine in the country, fought each other for control of territories. Drug-related homicides skyrocketed and hospital emergency rooms were filled with the maimed victims of the drug wars.

and-burgundy trim on the waist and neck) and leather moccasins called "docksiders."

The style suggested wealth, echoing leisure activities of the rich such as sailing, golf, and tennis. Because it became accessible to almost any consumer in mall stores such as J.C. Penney or The Gap, it lost some of its impact. Shopping by mail was common in the 1980s, and catalogues such as those of J. Crew and L. L. Bean also stocked preppy clothes for those who could not or did not want to spend the money on an "authentic" polo shirt from American fashion designer Ralph Lauren's collection.

Far removed from the preppy style was the fashion trend of taking clothes worn by America's youth and adding a designer touch. Street fashion became high fashion. Oversized clothing, stone-washed and acid-washed jeans, T-shirts, leather, and multiple ear piercings, once limited to youth, were in the mainstream of adult fashion by the end of the decade. Women began to combine the street-inspired look of ripped jeans or gel-spiked hair with the more elegant yuppie style of a blazer and Chanel bag (or other such combinations) in a merging of the styles characteristic of the late 1980s.

That same year, a sinister new form of cocaine appeared on the streets of American cites: crack. Crack was an easily made, smokable form of cocaine that was much cheaper and far more addictive than powder cocaine. It spread quickly and disastrously through inner-city neighborhoods. Young, poor minority males saw dealing the drug as a means to escape the ghetto. Crack was seen as the aggravating cause in the rise of domestic violence, child abuse, homelessness, school violence, and dropout rates across America.

In response to the growing drug crisis in the country, President Ronald Reagan established the Office of National Drug Control Policy in 1988. Its director became known as the nation's "drug czar." Nationwide, the "war on drugs" became a principal topic of discussion and concern. The U.S. Congress passed stiffer drug laws, and the federal government tried harder to prevent the smuggling of cocaine into the country. Eventually, U.S. military forces were sent to capture Colombian "drug lords" and to destroy their coca crops (cocaine is extracted from the leaves of the coca plant).

Inspired by the musical styles of punk and rap, this fashion attitude was in direct opposition to that of wearing a certain style of clothes in an effort to show off one's wealth. The objective with street fashion was to look as if one did not have money to spend on clothes or just did not care how one looked. Oversized clothes were part of the trend that included old jeans, men's undershirts, thrift-shop overcoats, and dark sunglasses. Young people purposely tore their shirts or treated their jeans with bleach or acid to give them a lived-in or old look.

Eventually this ragged, low-cost look caught on and entered the mainstream and became a sign of spendable income, as demonstrated by the widespread popularity of acid-washed jeans. These worn-looking jeans sold in catalogues and mall stores for as much as, and in many cases far more than, new-looking jeans. Faded denim in pants, skirts, and jackets became stylish and even chic as American designers began to offer this look in their collections.

❖ THE HOMELESS CRISIS

After the Great Society social programs of President Lyndon B. Johnson (1908–1973) in the 1960s, many Americans believed that homelessness was no longer a serious problem in the United States. In the 1980s, however, the number of homeless Americans grew dramatically, and their plight came to be recognized as one of the leading social problems of the decade. Homeless people, often called street people, became an increasingly frequent sight in New York, Los Angeles, Chicago, Washington, D.C., and many other major cities.

Men and women of all ages, individuals and families from varied backgrounds and circumstances, shabbily dressed and hungry, began roaming city streets, sleeping on benches in summer and on heating grates or in crowded public shelters in winter. Estimates of the number of homeless people ranged from three hundred thousand to as many as three million. Because, by definition, the homeless had no permanent addresses at which they could be contacted and counted, statistics were never reliable. Most social observers believed that the number of homeless individuals grew in the decade by almost 25 percent per year.

Homelessness has been a problem throughout American history, particularly after the rise of industrialization in the nineteenth century. Experts who grappled with the problem in the early 1980s found it hard to

Homeless people became an increasingly frequent sight on the streets of major cities during the 1980s. Reproduced by permission of the Corbis Corporation.

Hands Across America

In a human chain stretching from New York City to Long Beach, California, more than five million people grasped hands on May 25, 1986, to focus the nation's attention on and raise money for poverty, hunger, and homelessness. Hands Across America stretched more than four thousand miles across sixteen states and through five hundred cities. Celebrities such as comedian and actor Bill Cosby, filmmaker Steven Spielberg, and singer Frank Sinatra took part in the event as both planners and participants. Although organizers hoped to raise fifty million dollars, only thirty-three million was donated. After expenses, only sixteen million dollars remained for distribution to groups aiding the poor and the homeless.

explain why the homeless population in America had grown so large and why it had grown so suddenly. The debate about the causes of this homelessness was politically charged and never fully resolved. Almost all participants agreed, however, that no single cause lay behind the crisis.

Most supporters of the homeless were fierce critics of the administration of President Ronald Reagan (1911–). They believed his economic and social policies were one of the main reasons for the rising crisis. They blamed cuts in social-welfare programs such as Aid to Families with Dependent Children (AFDC) for pushing many individuals into the position of being unable to make rent payments. Critics of the Republican administration also condemned dramatic cuts in federal assistance for subsidized low-income housing.

At the same time, most people agreed that other economic forces also contributed to the homeless problem. For example, some of the homeless were working people whose low wages, frequently from minimum-wage jobs, did not allow them to keep up with the rising cost of living, much less the rising price of housing. Experts also pointed to a continuing nationwide decline in manufacturing jobs, which in many cases forced displaced workers to take lower-wage positions.

As homelessness grew in the 1980s, many groups worked on behalf of the homeless, urging federal officials to take measures to ease their burden. The U.S. Congress held hearings about the homeless crisis and passed several pieces of legislation. The most significant act authorized the spending of $1 billion in 1987 and 1988 (only six hundred million dollars was actually set aside) and included twenty provisions for homeless aid, including emergency-shelter funds, health care, and job training. President Reagan reluctantly signed this bill into law in 1987.

As the decade progressed, though, so did the crisis. Despite increased national awareness of the problem and various legislative and charitable efforts, the number of homeless people remained large. By decade's end, while the nature of the crisis and its possible solutions continued to be debated, public interest in the issue began to diminish.

❖ FOCUSING ON CHILD ABUSE

Child abuse arose as a serious social issue in the 1980s. It generated intense media attention, heightened public concern, congressional hearings, numerous books and articles, and increased workloads for child-protective-service (CPS) agencies. In 1984, the American Humane Association (AHA) estimated that there were 1.7 million abused or neglected children in the United States. Although experts disagreed about the total numbers of abused children, there was broad agreement among professionals that the problem in America was widespread and probably growing.

One factor that helped to account for the increase in reported cases was that nearly all states at the beginning of the decade required social-service professionals who had contact with children to report any case of suspected child abuse. Among reported cases of child mistreatment, neglect was found to be the largest problem, representing 63 percent of all cases. This was followed closely by cases of physical abuse and sexual abuse.

Public concern about the issue of child abuse was inflamed by news of sexual-abuse charges against adults in the Boy Scouts of America organization and against the clergy of various religious groups. Several highly publicized cases, including the McMartin Preschool sexual-abuse case, increased nationwide concern about the safety of nursery schools and day-care centers.

In 1984, teachers at the McMartin Preschool, a well-known, highly respected preschool in the upscale community of Manhattan Beach, not far from Los Angeles, were accused of sexually abusing children in their care. According to the criminal charges brought against seven teachers at the school, during a period of years, hundreds of three-, four-, and five-year-old children had been sexually abused, sometimes in bizarre rituals. Shortly after these allegations became public, claims surfaced that similar abuse had occurred at other preschools in the area. The shocking charges in the McMartin trial made national headlines, and the case became a national obsession. Seven years after it started, the McMartin trial, the longest in U.S. history, ended with the acquittal (found not guilty) of all the defendants. Despite the verdict, many people believed sexual abuse had occurred at the preschool.

To help stem the tide of child abuse, efforts were made to educate children to the signs and dangers of possible abuse. Board games such as Strangers and Dangers and Safe City, U.S.A., as well as various flashcards and coloring books flooded the market. Saturday-morning cartoon shows featured public service announcements warning children not to get into strangers' cars. At some schools, children attended classes instructing them what to do if someone tried to fondle them sexually. Some psychologists thought these methods were useful to educate children and their parents about important issues, but some disagreed, believing the methods only terrified many children.

❖ THE ANTINUCLEAR MOVEMENT

In the early 1980s, the idea of a nuclear war with the Soviet Union began to haunt the American public more forcefully than at any time since the Cuban missile crisis of October 1962 (a thirteen-day period when the United States and Russia came to the brink of nuclear war over the placement of Soviet nuclear missiles in Cuba). Warning of a threat by the Soviet military and calling the Soviet Union "the focus of evil in the world," President Ronald Reagan (1911–) oversaw a military buildup of over $1 trillion that specifically included new generations of nuclear weapons. At the same time, the Soviet Union continued to add aggressively to its own nuclear arsenal.

In the United States, defense officials spoke of fighting a "protracted" nuclear war, while military strategists suggested nuclear war was "winnable." In a 1983 Gallup poll, 40 percent of those Americans questioned thought it likely a nuclear war would occur within ten years. In November of the same year, when ABC broadcast *The Day After,* a fictional dramatization of a nuclear attack on Kansas City, one hundred million Americans tuned in.

Angered by the accelerating arms race in a world where fifty thousand nuclear warheads already existed, many people began to protest the military policies of the Reagan administration and the Soviet leadership. Spearheaded by existing groups such as the Committee for a Sane Nuclear Policy (SANE), the growing antinuclear movement brought together new peace organizations at local and state levels. The movement won the support of activists and volunteers from all walks of life and in all areas of the country.

*A demonstrator
protesting the dumping
of nuclear waste from the
Three Mile Island Nuclear
Power Plant into a
Baltimore river.* © *Lowell
Georgia/Corbis. Reproduced by
permission of the
Corbis Corporation.*

One popular proposal of these groups called for an immediate halt to the arms race, a "freeze" on all nuclear weapons testing, production, and deployment. Once the freezing of arms levels was achieved by both superpowers, proponents called for determined arms-control negotiations. In 1982, public-opinion polls showed that a weapons freeze was supported by 70 percent of Americans. Freeze propositions were placed on many state ballots and approved in some states. The freeze movement also won the support members of the U.S. Congress, as well as distinguished diplomats.

Antinuclear activists held rallies, lobbied Congress, supported profreeze candidates for public office, sponsored public seminars, published books and articles, and spoke on television and radio. Prominent in the movement were such well-known peace activists as pediatrician Benjamin Spock (1903–1998) and physicist Linus Pauling (1901–1994). Members of the antinuclear movement also opposed the building of new nuclear power plants in the United States.

The Reagan administration paid little attention to the antinuclear movement, except to suggest it was wrong. The administration never supported the idea of a nuclear freeze, arguing that it would lock the Soviet Union in a position of nuclear superiority. Reagan believed the only way to achieve serious arms control with the Soviet Union was to show an unwavering determination to continue the U.S. nuclear buildup. After Mikhail Gorbachev (1931–) came to power in the Soviet Union in 1985, tensions between the United States and the Soviet Union lessened. Subsequent negotiations between Gorbachev and Reagan produced nuclear-arms treaties, substantially reducing the threat of nuclear war.

❖ THE EVANGELICAL MOVEMENT AND THE WORLD OF POLITICS

The growth of evangelicalism and fundamentalism in the 1980s was a religious phenomenon that extended into American culture and politics. Known by many names (born-again Christians, evangelicals, Pentecostals, the New Religious Right) these Christians, mostly Protestants, grew in numbers like no single Protestant denomination.

Evangelicals are Protestants actively involved in converting others to their religious beliefs. They have conservative beliefs toward religion and issues of morality, they may or may not interpret the Bible literally, and they are not opposed to interacting with other Christian churches. A survey taken in 1986 showed that 31 percent of Americans identified themselves as evangelicals. The leading evangelical preachers of the era were Jimmy Swaggart, Jim Bakker, Oral Roberts, and Robert Schuller.

Fundamentalists are militant evangelicals. They believe modern society is sinful, interpret the Bible literally, and separate themselves from other Christian groups that do not completely share their beliefs. The premier fundamentalist preachers of the era were Jerry Falwell, James Robison, and Marion "Pat" Robertson.

Fundamentalists actively pursued an entrance into the world of American politics in the 1980s. In 1979, televangelist (television preacher) and fundamentalist Jerry Falwell had founded the Moral Majority, a religious organization whose goal was to mobilize Christian believers for conservative political purposes. The Moral Majority formed chapters and local affiliates in all fifty states and sought to register conservative or Republican voters. Its aim was to influence elections, support conservative candidates, and combat liberal or Democratic groups whom, it believed, had come to dominate the nation.

Jimmy Swaggart, one of the leading evangelical preachers of the 1980s.
Reproduced by permission of AP/Wide World Photos.

Joining Falwell in his crusade to change the moral views of American politics was Marion "Pat" Robertson. A televangelist and head of the Christian Broadcasting Network, Robertson announced in October 1987 his intention to run for the Republican presidential nomination the following year. Although he garnered some support, mostly from conservative Christians, Robertson was labeled an extremist by his opponents for his religious solutions to the cultural problems of the nation. He failed to win the nomination, but did help strengthen the conservative religious forces in the Republican Party.

As televangelists and fundamentalists assumed higher public roles, they also came under greater public scrutiny. Many were criticized for their million-dollar empires and lavish lifestyles. Some, like Jim Bakker, head of the PTL (Praise the Lord or People That Love) empire, were forced to resign when news of their adulterous affairs and theft were revealed. In 1989, Bakker was sent to prison for having defrauded his followers of more than $158 million.

❖ THE NEW AGE MOVEMENT

The New Age movement was not a religion as much as it was a blend of several Eastern philosophies. Initially somewhat of a fringe movement, New Age broke into the mainstream in the mid-1980s and soon found its

The Harmonic Convergence

No single event symbolized the New Age movement of the 1980s more than the Harmonic Convergence. The Convergence was marked by a gathering of 144,000 people at more than 350 so-called sacred locations around the planet on August 16 and 17, 1987. Its goal was to generate a universal energy that would help create world peace and harmony. The rituals of dance, prayer, and prophecy were expected to reach out to the stars and attract extraterrestrial powers that would help people on Earth achieve peace.

The Convergence was organized by José Argüelles, an art historian from Colorado, who came up with the idea for the event after studying ancient Mayan and Aztec calendars. He claimed to have found patterns, or "great cycles," that occurred throughout the ages where Earth sent out a beacon to the stars and rejuvenated itself. He calculated that the time had come for another one of these great cycles. The Convergence drew media attention as well as ridicule from people in and out of the movement. In the end, no extraterrestrials were spotted at the Convergence, but followers still believed the power that they had unleashed in the two-day event would benefit the world.

way into contemporary society in several ways. New Age music, speakers, and books became readily available across the United States as stores selling New Age materials multiplied. New Age became an immensely profitable endeavor, as well as a somewhat contradictory one. The contradictions arose because the movement's teachings of individuality, oneness with nature, and simple lifestyles clashed with its commercial obsession and use of the media and celebrities. Curiously, the movement was easily accepted by Americans, many of whom either already belonged to an established church or professed no religious belief at all.

The New Age movement avoided specific religious beliefs, but some of its basic principles included a belief in reincarnation, spiritual healing, out-of-body experiences, meditation, yoga, astrology, and some belief in the supernatural or extraterrestrial. The movement was not truly new in many senses because it borrowed from several earlier mystical or occult teachings. Native American Shamanism, early Christianity, and the counterculture or youth culture of the 1960s all played prominent roles in the movement.

Its largest influence, however, stemmed from Eastern religious traditions. Buddhism and Hinduism provided much of the structure of the new movement. Early New Age pioneers, such as Marilyn Ferguson, presented these various spiritual approaches in a simplified form to an American audience. Ferguson's 1980 book, *The Aquarian Conspiracy,* touched a chord in the American public because it gave a modern interpretation to ideas and mystic concepts that people had believed in for centuries. Surveys done in the late 1980s showed that about thirty million, or one in four, American adults believed in the idea of reincarnation. The movement exploded in 1987 when actress Shirley Maclaine brought her own story of New Age reincarnation to television in a miniseries.

Humanity acting as its own god was the core New Age belief. Preaching a message of self-love, New Age gurus stressed that every man, woman, and child was a spiritual entity and was interconnected with one another. They went so far as to claim that all people and nations, past and present, were interconnected in the cosmos. New Agers held political views that were primarily liberal to radical. A call to end nationalism (excessive devotion to a particular nation), opposition to nuclear weapons, and expansion of environmental awareness formed the core politics of believers.

The New Age movement was not a cult or an organized church because it possessed few temples or official places of worship. Instead, the movement was unified by an optimistic, simple message that appealed to millions of Americans in one version or another. The appeal of nonthreatening rituals, such as meditation and yoga, as well as celebrity endorsements drew in hundreds of eager participants.

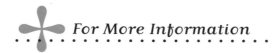

For More Information

BOOKS

Bibb, Porter. *Ted Turner: It Ain't as Easy as It Looks.* Boulder, CO: Johnson Books, 1997.

Birnbach, Lisa, ed. *The Official Preppy Handbook.* New York: Workman Publications, 1980.

Carroll, Marilyn. *Cocaine and Crack.* Berkeley Heights, NJ: Enslow Publishers, 1994.

Ferguson, Marilyn. *The Aquarian Conspiracy: Personal and Social Transformation in the 1980s.* New York: St. Martin's Press, 1980.

Freedman, Suzanne. *Vanessa Williams.* Broomall, PA: Chelsea House, 1999.

Martin, William. *With God on Our Side: The Rise of the Religious Right in America.* New York: Broadway Books, 1996.

Schell, Jonathon. *The Fate of the Earth.* New York: Knopf, 1982.

Steele, Shelby. *The Content of Our Character: A New Vision of Race in America.* New York: St. Martin's Press, 1990.

WEB SITES

The 80s Server. http://www.80s.com/cgi-bin/80smain.cgi (accessed on July 29, 2002).

National Clearinghouse on Child Abuse and Neglect Information. http://www.calib.com/nccanch/ (accessed on July 29, 2002).

National Coalition for the Homeless. http://www.nationalhomeless.org/ (accessed on July 29, 2002).

Rubik's Online Home Page. http://www.rubiks.com/ (accessed on July 29, 2002).

Yesterdayland-Fashion from the 80s. http://www.yesterdayland.com/popopedia/shows/decades/fashion_1980s.php (accessed on July 29, 2002).

Medicine and Health

1980: The World Health Organization formally announces the worldwide elimination of smallpox.

1980: June 6 A U.S. Senate subcommittee is told of a baffling, recently discovered disease called toxic shock syndrome that frequently strikes young women and can cause death within a few days.

1980: September 22 Rely brand tampons are recalled because federal studies link their use to increased risks of toxic shock syndrome.

1981: January 8 Scientific studies confirm a long-term advantage in reducing cholesterol and saturated fats in the fight against heart disease.

1981: January 13 A three-month study links toxic shock syndrome to the use of high-absorbency tampons and confirms that teenagers have the highest risk of developing the disease.

1981: June A new disease that will come to be known as acquired immunodeficiency syndrome (AIDS) is first detected among homosexual men and intravenous drug users.

1982: September 29 The first of seven people die in Chicago after taking Extra-Strength Tylenol painkilling capsules tainted with cyanide.

1982: December 2 Physicians at the University of Utah Medical Center in Salt Lake City successfully implant a permanent artificial heart in a sixty-one-year-old patient.

1982: December 9 The Centers for Disease Control and Prevention in Atlanta announce that AIDS is now spreading to infants and children.

1983: January 25 A study by the Food Resource and Action Center links an eight-state increase in infant mortality to poverty brought on by the economic recession.

1983: May 24 AIDS is called the nation's "number one priority" of the U.S. Public Health Service.

1984: February 16 The American Heart Association, American Lung Association, and American Cancer Society denounce cigarette ads.

1984: April 21 The Centers for Disease Control and Prevention confirm news reports that French researchers have identified a virus thought to be the cause of AIDS.

1984: **October 26** Doctors in Loma Linda, California, replace the defective heart of a newborn baby girl known as "Baby Fae" with the heart of a baboon.

1985: **February 17** A third permanent artificial heart is implanted at Humana Hospital in Louisville, Kentucky.

1985: **June** The Renfrew Center, the first residential facility devoted exclusively to the treatment of the eating disorders anorexia nervosa and bulimia, is opened in Philadelphia.

1985: **September 9** New York City school districts are struck by a boycott when a seven-year-old AIDS victim is given permission to attend school.

1986: **May** An international commission names the AIDS-causing virus the human immunodeficiency virus or HIV.

1986: **June 30** The federal government announces $100 million in contracts to step up research for a cure for AIDS.

1986: **September 19** The federal government announces that an experimental drug, azidothymidine (AZT), prolonged the lives of some AIDS victims.

1987: **March 20** The U.S. Food and Drug Administration approves the marketing of AZT in the United States for treating symptoms of AIDS.

1987: **May 31** President Ronald Reagan refuses entry into the United States immigrants and aliens with AIDS.

1987: **October 11** The AIDS quilt is unfurled for the first time on the Mall in Washington, D.C.

1988: **May 12** The National Institutes of Health halt funding for artificial-heart programs, citing failures for all five patients who had received them.

1988: **June 1** The National Academy of Sciences criticizes the absence of strong federal leadership and support in the fight against AIDS.

1988: **June 27** Michigan becomes the first state to outlaw surrogate-mother contracts.

1989: **March 8** The U.S. Department of Health and Human Services says it will support programs to supply hypodermic needles to drug addicts to help halt the spread of AIDS.

1989: **June 1** A *New England Journal of Medicine* article reports that the AIDS virus can lie dormant for up to three years before it is detected with standard blood tests.

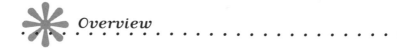

Overview

A deadly epidemic disease, AIDS (acquired immunodeficiency syndrome), marked the 1980s for Americans more than any other medical or health news. First reported in 1981, AIDS is brought about by the human immunodeficiency virus (HIV), which attacks selected cells in the immune system. This renders the body unable to resist disease-causing organisms and certain cancers. Americans were profoundly shocked by AIDS. The disease at first seemed to affect predominantly homosexual and bisexual men. But the medical community soon found that intravenous drug users, hemophiliacs (people suffering from a blood disease in which their blood fails to clot), recipients of blood transfusions, and any sexual partner of an AIDS victim were also at risk. AIDS spread rapidly until almost 1.5 million Americans were estimated to be infected with the virus by the end of the decade.

Americans, with their great faith in scientific technology, assumed medicine would soon provide a quick fix to the disease. But by 1989, no cure or vaccine existed for AIDS. Many of those infected were not even aware they carried the virus and could spread it. Problems with their immune systems might not become apparent for years because of the long gestation period of the virus. The medical and social costs of the disease were enormous. Because of its early association with homosexual behavior, AIDS acquired a stigma that further complicated identification and treatment. Public hysteria led to children who were AIDS patients being banned from schools. Victims were shunned by family, friends, neighbors, and even some medical personnel.

In the absence of effective medical technology against AIDS, prevention and education were the only weapons. In 1988, after years of controversy, the U.S. Public Health Service mailed a comprehensive and straightforward brochure to every American household that emphasized preventive measures against the epidemic. By 1989, the physical, economic, and social tolls of AIDS were still increasing. Scientists, the medical community, and others continued to address the problem, and Americans continued to hope for a solution.

Many of the technological and social issues in medicine and health in the 1980s came to be symbolized by Americans with the names Barney Clark, Baby Fae, and Baby M. The most widely publicized medical technology of the decade was the artificial heart program. Until the program was halted in 1990, many Americans followed the progress of patients such as Barney Clark as he struggled to live after receiving a permanent artificial heart. Medical technology had also progressed to the point where a physician tried to save a doomed newborn, Baby Fae, by transplanting the heart from a different species into her chest. Reproductive technology gave many couples who could not bear children new hopes, as in the case of Baby M and her surrogate mother. All these cases presented new ethical and legal issues, in addition to disappointment and heartache.

Americans were shaken from their complacent faith in over-the-counter health-care products by several cases of product tampering and product failure in the decade. In 1982, an unidentified person murdered seven people in the Chicago area by filling Tylenol gelcaps with cyanide and placing the product boxes back on store shelves. After several other copycat episodes of product tampering, the industry was forced to redo both gelatin capsules and product containers, creating elaborate protective devices. Lawsuits over toxic-shock-causing superabsorbent tampons forced manufacturers to withdraw such products from the market.

The decade was marked by a recognition of diseases and psychological conditions to which Americans had previously given little thought: Alzheimer's disease, anorexia nervosa, and bulimia. As the number of older Americans increased in the 1980s, so did the frequency and severity of the memory-robbing Alzheimer's disease, which received increasing attention both in the medical community and the media. The two eating disorders, anorexia nervosa and bulimia, were extreme examples of an American society obsessed with dieting and appearance. Poorly understood during the 1980s, they proved puzzling and frustrating to health workers and to the families of those who suffered from the disorders.

William DeVries (1943–) William DeVries and his surgical team at the University of Utah Medical Center made medical history and national headlines on December 2, 1982, when they replaced the diseased heart of Barney Clark with the Jarvik-7, the first permanent artificial heart ever used for a human patient. DeVries was the only surgeon authorized at the time by the U.S. Food and Drug Administration (FDA) to implant an artificial heart into a human. Before the FDA ended the innovative artificial-heart program in 1990, DeVries had performed four such transplants. *Photo reproduced by permission of AP/Wide World Photos.*

Robert Gallo (1937–) Robert Gallo and his research team at the National Cancer Institute (NCI) claimed to have identified in 1983 the human T-cell lymphotropic virus type III (HTLV-III). The following year, he and his colleagues published their findings in *Science*. Gallo and the other scientists in his laboratory developed a blood test for the virus. Although Gallo and others continued to search for a cure, by decade's end the medical solution to the deadly, slow-acting, changing virus still remained a scientific mystery. *Photo reproduced by permission of Archive Photos, Inc.*

C. Everett Koop (1916–) In 1981, C. Everett Koop became surgeon general of the United States, the nation's leading spokesperson on public-health issues. During his eight-year term, he stood out as a model of integrity and courage in public office, promoting the nation's medical interests over party politics. In 1982, Koop took a hard stand against smoking and the tobacco industry. Addressing the issue of AIDS, he spoke graphically and candidly about safe and unsafe sex practices. Disregarding the Reagan administration, which had appointed him, Koop argued for intensive sex education in the nation's schools. *Photo reproduced by permission of Archive Photos, Inc.*

Ryan White (1971–1990) Ryan White contracted AIDS in 1984 through tainted blood products he was given to treat hemophilia, an inherited blood disease in which the blood does not clot properly, causing excessive bleeding. The following year, he was denied the right to attend school. He and his family took the school district to court, and his successful legal battle made headlines all over the world. Confronted with continued discrimination, White kept up his campaign against widespread ignorance and fear of AIDS throughout the rest of the decade, becoming a celebrity in the process. *Photo reproduced by permission of UPI/Corbis-Bettmann.*

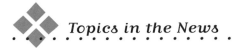

Topics in the News . . . .

❖ AIDS

In the late 1970s, a rare form of cancer called Kaposi's sarcoma and an unusual type of pneumonia called *Pneumocystis carinii* began to appear in previously healthy homosexual and bisexual men in the United States. What was disturbing to health officials was the fact that the patients' immune systems were not functioning properly, causing them to be susceptible to diseases that would not normally occur in a healthy person. Also, the form of pneumonia these men had contracted was so rare that even a few cases in a single year made it definable as an epidemic.

The Centers for Disease Control and Prevention (CDC), the federal epidemiology agency in Atlanta, made its first official announcement of the new, unidentified illnesses on June 5, 1981. (The CDC researches health problems and works to prevent and to control the spread of disease.) The CDC informed the medical community of the fatal nature of the new illnesses and highly unusual spread of the normally rare Kaposi's sarcoma among young homosexual men (Kaposi's sarcoma was usually limited to the elderly). Since the first cases in the United States seemed to affect only homosexuals, the U.S. Public Health Service named the complex of diseases GRID: gay-related immune deficiency. When heterosexuals began to become victims also, GRID became known as acquired immunodeficiency syndrome, or AIDS.

This destruction of the body's immune system also began to be seen among intravenous drug users, people who had received blood transfusions, and sexual partners of people who had the disease. It was soon determined that AIDS was caused by a virus that could be passed from person to person through contact with blood or bodily fluids. The disease can be transmitted through semen or vaginal fluids during unprotected sex with an infected person and through direct contact with infected blood. Intravenous drug users who share hypodermic needles are at an especially high risk. AIDS can also be passed from an infected mother to her unborn child.

In 1983, the virus believed to cause AIDS was discovered and named HTLV-III (human T-cell lymphotropic virus type III). Its name was soon changed to human immunodeficiency virus or HIV. HIV damages the immune system by attacking certain white blood cells called lymphocytes (specifically those called helper T cells), which normally help to protect the body against invading microorganisms. When these cells are destroyed, the body loses its ability to fight infection and becomes vulnerable to a variety of diseases and rare cancers that are the hallmarks of AIDS.

Top Causes of Death in America: 1985

Cause	Number
1. Heart disease	771, 169
2. Cancer	461,563
3. Stroke	153,050
4. Accidents	93,457
5. Lung disease	74,662
6. Influenza and pneumonia	67,615
7. Diabetes	36,969
8. Suicide	29,453
9. Liver disease	26,767
10. Arteriosclerosis	23,926

The AIDS epidemic spread rapidly after 1982. While ten new cases a week were diagnosed that year, one hundred cases a week were diagnosed just two years later. By the end of 1988, the total number of AIDS cases reported to the CDC numbered eighty-six thousand. Many physicians realized that they were in the midst of a major medical problem. Public fears fueled by media reports led to a kind of collective hysteria, but public health agencies and the federal government moved very slowly against the disease.

There were two primary reasons for the federal government's reluctance to confront the issue. First, the diseases associated with AIDS were rare enough that there were relatively few trained physicians and medical researchers who were familiar with them. Second, the first patients with AIDS were primarily homosexual men, and the administration of President Ronald Reagan (1911–) was uncomfortable with the link between the spread of AIDS and homosexual behavior. Critics believe that by not addressing the issue more aggressively, the White House lost valuable time in helping the public to understand how AIDS could be transmitted and further fueled public panic as well as a backlash against the gay community. In the early years of the crisis, the federal government's research teams saw AIDS as a budget problem and did not provide major funding for AIDS research until the epidemic had spread to people throughout all walks of life across the country.

Fear and rejection of the victims complicated the nation's ability to deal with the deadly disease. Since the earliest victims identified as AIDS

Poisoned Tylenol

In 1982, the nation was shocked by the news that seven Chicago-area residents had died after taking Extra-Strength Tylenol capsules that an unknown person had laced with cyanide, a poisonous salt. The incident led to a rash of copycat poisonings of other food and drug products, including Extra-Strength Tylenol laced with strychnine (a poisonous plant product) in California, mouthwash tainted with hydrochloric acid in Florida, and cold medicines, allergy remedies, and appetite suppressants spiked with rat poison in other areas of the country.

In response, the U.S. Food and Drug Administration (FDA) ordered tamper-resistant packaging for over-the-counter drugs. Tylenol manufacturer Johnson & Johnson exceeded the FDA packaging requirements with a triple safety seal. But in early 1986, a twenty-three-year-old woman died of cyanide poisoning in New York after she took two capsules from a freshly opened bottle.

Johnson & Johnson pulled Tylenol from store shelves and announced that it was discontinuing the manufacture and sale of the capsule form of its drugs. Instead, Tylenol would be produced only as tablets and caplets, tablets that were capsule-shaped and coated to make swallowing easier. Both the American people and American corporations had to make new adaptations to face the uncertain and often dangerous of the world of the 1980s.

sufferers were homosexual males and intravenous drug users, some people who held strict moral views believed the disease was a form of punishment for the victims' "sins." Misinformation was common. A 1985 poll revealed that about half of all Americans believed AIDS could be transmitted through casual contact, such as sharing a drinking glass. It could not. The fatal nature of the disease also terrified and panicked people. Schoolchildren with AIDS were rejected, and attempts were made either to keep them out of school or to isolate them from their classmates.

The announcement in July 1985 that film actor Rock Hudson had AIDS (he died on October 2, 1985) dramatically increased public awareness of the crisis, but many problems remained unsolved. Debates over whether to isolate patients led to controversies. Efforts to protect public health led to discrimination against foreign visitors or potential immigrants. Those testing positive for AIDS were not permitted to enter the country. Some victims of the disease found it difficult to get adequate health insurance coverage because of the high expense of treating patients. The slow process of the U.S. Food and Drug Administration (FDA) for approval of new AIDS drugs caused AIDS activists to demand that the government speed up the process by postponing some of the required testing.

By 1989, there was still no vaccine to protect against HIV infection, nor were there many major drugs to prolong and ease the lives of victims. AZT (azidothymidine) was one drug licensed by the FDA for AIDS patients. It interfered with virus replication, prolonging life for many years in some patients and delaying the onset of "full-blown" AIDS in people with no symptoms. But for some, it had harmful and toxic side effects, including nausea, vomiting, loss of red and white blood cells, and muscle pain and weakness.

Since no vaccines or effective lifesaving therapies were available during the decade, federal health officials tried to educate the public on ways to reduce the risk of contracting the disease. In 1988, the U.S. Public Health Service issued a candid brochure about HIV infection and AIDS based on the surgeon general's report. Every household in America received it in the mail. "Safe sex," meaning sex using AIDS-preventive measures, became a common phrase even as controversies arose over providing condoms for high-school-age children instead of encouraging sexual abstinence. The question of providing clean needles to drug addicts to prevent the spread of AIDS also created controversy.

By the end of the 1980s, AIDS was still spreading in the United States and the rest of the world. Despite efforts to create new weapons against the disease, it still baffled scientists and the medical community. Some infected with HIV were without symptoms, and some AIDS victims lived throughout the decade with the disease, raising hopes that information could be found from their ability to fight off the disease. By 1989, scientists felt that while they might not be able to cure the disease, they might find some additional therapies that could keep the AIDS virus in check without the side effects of treatments like AZT.

❖ THE FIRST ARTIFICIAL HEART

The first successful artificial heart procedure took place in 1957 when Dr. Willem Kolff and Tetsuzu Akutsu of the Cleveland Clinic developed a heart that kept a dog alive for one and a half hours. Researchers spent the next several decades developing four-chambered hearts for temporary use

Tampons and Toxic Shock

After 344 cases of a rare and baffling illness that came to be known as toxic shock syndrome were reported in 1980, the Centers for Disease Control and Prevention (CDC) linked women's use of tampons to the outbreak of the sometimes fatal syndrome. One study of a group of sufferers discovered that 71 percent of them had used Procter & Gamble's Rely tampons. Procter & Gamble ordered a recall of its tampons and soon found itself in court.

Toxic shock syndrome (TSS) is a severe illness associated with infection by the bacterium *Staphylococcus aureus*. The CDC found it occurred most commonly in menstruating women who used tampons (about 75 percent of TSS victims) although it also occurred in children, men, and nonmenstruating women. Up to 5 percent of the cases are fatal. The syndrome has a sudden onset with high fever, vomiting, diarrhea, and a sunburnlike red rash that could occur anywhere on the body. Within a day or two, victims can suffer a drop in blood pressure, ranging from mild symptoms of dizziness to fatal shock. Treatment includes intensive antibiotic therapy.

Studies of Rely and other tampons indicated that certain types of superabsorbing tampons contained cellulose chips that absorbed magnesium, which acted as a nutrient to encourage the growth of *Staphylococcus aureus*. The bacteria, in turn, generated poisonous waste products, which were circulated by the blood. Hundred of lawsuits were brought on behalf of victims who suffered brain damage, gangrene, partial paralysis, and death. The superabsorbing products were removed from the market, and materials educating menstruating women about the safe use of tampons were distributed.

in humans. The first artificial heart intended as a permanent replacement for a diseased human heart was the Jarvik-7, developed by Robert K. Jarvik, a physician working in the artificial-organs division of the University of Utah Medical Center. It consisted of compressed-air tubes leading outside the chest to a power source and was first widely tested on animals. Among the more than one hundred calves, sheep, and goats receiving the artificial heart, three had strokes related to infections.

After the U.S. Food and Drug Administration (FDA) granted approval for human use, the Jarvik-7 was first implanted on December 2, 1982, into

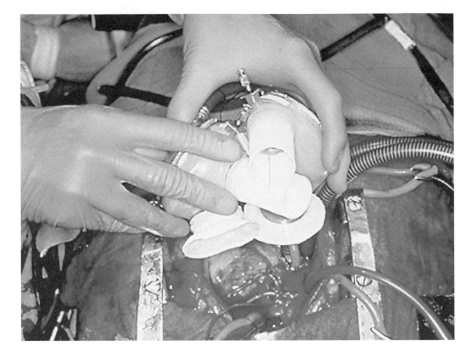

*Surgical implantation of a
Jarvik artificial heart.
©NIH, National Audubon
Society Collection/Photo
Researchers, Inc. Reproduced
by permission of Photo
Researchers, Inc.*

the chest of Barney Clark, a sixty-one-year-old retired dentist suffering
from a fatal disease of unknown cause that was destroying the muscles of
his heart. After many medical setbacks including seizures, pneumonia,
and nosebleeds, Clark finally died on March 23, 1983, of complications
from preexisting kidney and lung disease. The Jarvik-7 heart, however,
worked until the end, and its implantation was considered a success.

Over the next few years, four more patients received artificial heart
transplants. However, all eventually died. Three of the five suffered
strokes. Three of the five also died after relatively short periods. Barney
Clark lived 112 days after receiving his artificial heart. Murray Haydon
lived for sixteen months. William Schroeder survived the longest, living
for 620 days before a fourth stroke and lung infection led to his death.
Unlike the three experimental animals whose strokes were related to
infections, the human strokes were caused by blood clots that originally
formed in the heart and then traveled to the brain. Anticoagulants were
given to artificial-heart recipients to prevent their blood from clotting, but
the drugs produced other serious complications.

After these disturbing setbacks, physicians questioned the use of the
devices as permanent replacements and began to use them as a temporary
"bridge" for people awaiting a human heart transplant. Some patients did
not have a suitable donor heart immediately available or needed time to

Baby Fae and Her Baboon Heart

On November, 15, 1984, at Loma Linda University Medical Center in southern California, a tiny baby girl died twenty days after she had heart surgery. "Baby Fae," as she had come to be known, died with the heart of a baboon pumping blood through her body. The baboon heart experiment offered hope that animal organs could be used in ailing infants for whom transplant organs were difficult to obtain. Baby Fae was born with a fatal congenital deformity known as hypoplastic left heart, which left the entire left side of her heart useless. A successful transplant from a baboon promised a new life for Baby Fae and a revolution in pediatric heart surgery.

Leonard Bailey, the pediatric heart surgeon who had performed the surgery, had experimented with interspecies transplants for seven years, grafting lamb hearts into baby goats. For transplants between animals and humans, he chose baboons because of their biological similarity to humans. However, he made a grave error with Baby Fae by using a heart from a baboon with a different blood type. Baby Fae was given antirejection drugs so her body would not reject the foreign organ, but the strain on her body was too much, and she eventually died of kidney failure.

Controversy surrounded the entire operation, and the medical community was sharply divided. Many physicians challenged the use of an animal heart when a human heart seemed preferable. Animal rights groups protested the sacrifice of a healthy baboon for what they saw as medical sensationalism. Those concerned with medical morality worried about the ethical questions of consent for an infant in such a risky undertaking. Questions even arose about her psychological well-being once she was old enough to understand that the heart that beat within her chest was that of a baboon. In the end, many questions remained unanswered. The medical community and Americans across the nation would reflect on the case of Baby Fae for a long time to come.

recover from health conditions that made a transplant ill-advised. The first FDA-authorized temporary use of an artificial heart as a bridge to a human heart transplant occurred in August 1985 at the University of Arizona Medical Center in Tucson. There, a twenty-five-year-old Arizona man suffering from a severe viral heart infection awaited a new donor heart. Seven days after the surgery, he suffered a series of mild strokes, necessitating an urgent human heart transplant. His Jarvik-7 was later found to have blood clots on its left side, where the main pumping chamber joined the aorta (main artery of the body).

The artificial heart did prove potentially useful in a way its designers had not seen. Originally intended as a permanent replacement for a diseased heart, it became used more as a temporary bridge to keep patients alive until a human heart could be found for transplant. However, the procedure was enormously expensive, and many people raised the question whether such money might be better spent on prevention than on a risky and expensive procedure for one patient. Federal funding for the Jarvik-7 project stopped in 1988, and implantations were restricted to temporary use. On January 11, 1990, after reviewing the ongoing problems with the device, the FDA recalled the Jarvik-7 and forbade its further use in human patients.

❖ THE CASE OF "BABY M" AND SURROGATE MOTHERHOOD

Surrogate motherhood—in which a woman becomes pregnant and bears a child for another woman, often for payment—became news to most Americans in 1986 when the notorious case of "Baby M" made headlines. In most cases of surrogate motherhood, a married couple in which the husband was fertile but the wife was infertile or unable to carry a pregnancy, entered into a privately arranged contract with another woman. That women (the surrogate) agreed to be artificially inseminated with the sperm from the fertile husband and to carry the developing fetus to term. The contract usually called for restrictions on the surrogate mother's behavior during pregnancy and gave the husband of the married couple some authority to make medical decisions about her and the fetus. After giving birth, the surrogate assumed no parental rights, turning the baby over to the married couple according to the terms of the signed contract, which usually involved a large sum of money.

In 1985, Mary Beth Whitehead signed a contract agreeing to act as a surrogate mother for William and Elizabeth Stern for a payment of ten thousand dollars. When the baby was born on March 27, 1986 (a girl who came to be known to the public as Baby M), Whitehead felt she had made a terrible mistake. She named the infant Sara Elizabeth White-head, took her home, and turned down the ten thousand dollars. On March 30, the Sterns took the infant to their home. The baby was back at the Whitehead home the following day. During the second week of April, Whitehead told the Sterns she would never be able to give up her daughter. The Sterns responded by hiring an attorney to fight for the contract's enforcement. The police then removed Baby M from White-head's custody.

Whitehead then sued the Sterns in January 1987. After a well-publicized and prolonged custody battle, the lower New Jersey court upheld the contract, giving the child to the Sterns. Elizabeth Stern formally adopted the child, whom the Sterns named Melissa Elizabeth Stern. In 1988, however, the New Jersey Supreme Court reversed the previous ruling and banned surrogate contracts for pay. It gave custody of the child to William Stern, invalidated Elizabeth Stern's adoption of the child, and gave Mary Beth Whitehead broad visitation rights.

The Baby M case raised troubling questions. Should surrogacy be outlawed? Who was qualified to determine a child's "best interest"? Was a surrogate-mother contract baby-selling? At the end of the decade, answers to these and other questions were still being formulated. Many state legislatures began to regulate surrogate arrangement because of the large sums of money involved and the growing industry of surrogate-mother brokering. Some states legalized commercial surrogacy, passing laws that made couples who contracted for surrogacy services the legal parents of the children produced. Other states banned the procedure entirely.

Surrogate mother Mary Beth Whitehead, who fought an unsuccessful court battle for custody of the child she was paid to bear for another couple. **Reproduced by permission of Bettye Lane.**

❖ **RECOGNITION OF ALZHEIMER'S DISEASE**

Alzheimer's is an irreversible brain disease in which damaged and dying brain cells cause devastating mental deterioration over a period of time. Often confused with senility (mental and physical deterioration associated with old age), its symptoms include increasingly poor memory, personality changes, and loss of concentration and judgment. Victims reach a point where they are unable to speak, think, or care for themselves. Death usually occurs within ten years after diagnosis.

The disease is named after German neurologist Alois Alzheimer (1864–1915), who was the first to describe it. In 1906, he studied a fifty-one-year-old woman whose personality and mental abilities were obviously deteriorating: she forgot things, became paranoid, and acted strangely. After the woman's death, Alzheimer examined her brain and noted an unusual thickening and tangling of the organ's nerve fibers. He also found that the cell body and nucleus of nerve cells had disappeared. Alzheimer noted that these changes indicated some new, unidentified illness.

More than seven decades would pass before researchers again turned their attention to this puzzling, destructive malady. Before the 1980s,

An Alzheimer's patient in a nursing home being attended to by a geriatric social worker. Reproduced by permission of Martha Tabor/Working Images Photographs.

Doctors' Average Salaries: 1985

Specialty	Salary
Radiology	$135,000
Anesthesiology	$133,000
General surgery	$129,000
Obstetrics/Gynecology	$120,000
Internal medicine	$90,000
Psychiatry	$80,000
Family practice	$70,000
Pediatrics	$70,000

many Americans had never heard of Alzheimer's disease. Although many families watched their loved ones succumb to it, the disease did not become familiar to the public until the news broke in 1981 that legendary film star Rita Hayworth (1918–1987) suffered from Alzheimer's disease.

Researchers in the 1980s found treatments for the disease even more elusive than finding its cause. No wonder drug existed for the disease, nor even a clear and consistent treatment approach. Researchers found that some drugs helped some of the people some of the time, and each patient responded differently. Sadly, having a diagnosis and receiving treatment for Alzheimer's could not stop the disease; a person inevitably got worse. By 1989, much was known about the symptoms of the disease, but little was still known of the causes. Ongoing research attempted to unlock the secrets of the disease, but neither a full scientific understanding nor a cure existed.

Alzheimer's disease received considerable public attention during the 1980s. The media emphasized the impact the illness had on both its victims and their families. Most communities did not have services or care facilities developed specifically for the long-term needs of Alzheimer's patients, nor did they provide support services for the caregivers of those patients. But many communities did have agencies that provided for the various needs of the elderly, and by decade's end many of these agencies often provided support and service to both patients and their caregivers.

❖ THE RISE OF EATING DISORDERS

Eating disorders are psychological conditions that involve overeating, voluntary starvation, or both. The best-known eating disorders are probably anorexia nervosa and bulimia. Eating disorders are virtually unknown in parts of the world where food is scarce. They are also rarely seen in less prosperous groups in developed countries. Although these disorders have been documented throughout history, they gained national attention in the United States when Karen Carpenter, a member of the popular singing duo The Carpenters, died on February 4, 1983, from heart failure caused by chronic anorexia nervosa.

The word anorexia comes from the Greek adjective *anorektos,* which means "without appetite." Anorexia is a form of extreme self-starvation and distortion of body image. The problem for people suffering from anorexia is not that they are not hungry. They starve themselves out of fear of gaining weight, even when they are severely underweight. Their self-image is so distorted that they see themselves as fat even when they look almost like a skeleton. Some anorexics refuse to eat at all; others nibble only small portions of fruit and vegetables or live on diet drinks. In addition to fasting, anorexics may exercise strenuously to keep their weight abnormally low. The self-imposed starvation takes a heavy toll on the body. Muscles begin to waste away. Bones stop growing and become brittle. The heart weakens. Muscle cramps, dizziness, fatigue, and even brain damage and kidney and heart failure are possible. About 10 to 20 percent of anorexics die, either as a result of starvation or suicide.

In the 1980s, anorexia nervosa occurred mostly among adolescent women. As it became more common during the decade, estimates of its incidence were as high as one in one hundred teenage girls and young women. Unlike victims of many other psychological disorders, anorexics had many social traits in common. Anorexia was fifteen times more likely to be found in females than males, typically began in adolescence, and was most common in wealthier families.

Little known even by physicians before the 1980s, bulimia was first thought to be an aspect of anorexia nervosa. It gets its name from the Greek word *boulimos,* meaning "great hunger" or, literally, "the hunger of an ox." People suffering from bulimia go on eating binges, often gorging on junk food, then force their bodies to get rid of the food to prevent weight gain, either by making themselves vomit or by taking large amounts of laxatives.

Like anorexia, bulimia results in starvation. But there are behavioral, physical, and psychological differences between the two disorders. Bulimia is much more difficult to detect because people who suffer from the disorder tend to be of normal weight or may even be slightly overweight.

RSI: A New Injury for a New Age

With the rise of video games and computers in the 1980s came a new type of syndrome. The many aches and severe pains resulting from these activities became known as repetitive stress injury (RSI). Video-game players found themselves with an especially troublesome pain and swelling in the wrist caused by the rapid repetition of button pressing, paddle twisting, joystick pushing, sphere rolling, or combinations of these actions. An estimated 65 percent of all video-game fans suffered from RSI at some time.

However, most publicity went to injuries from computer use. According to the Bureau of Labor Statistics, RSI accounted for nearly half of all 1988 workplace illnesses in private industry, compared to only 18 percent in 1981. The big increase came from data processors and journalists who spent long hours at the keyboard. Working at a computer for lengths of time stressed the wrists, elbows, and shoulders. Tendons in the arm became inflamed, leading to numbness and pain. Unless the injuries were diagnosed and treated, they could develop into serious lifelong disabilities. The science of ergonomics, or how humans adapt to the workplace, came to the rescue with design alterations to minimize such problems. Experts said frequent short breaks from work were crucial, but the real key was to make technology adapt to humans instead of the other way around.

They tend to hide their habit of binge eating followed by purging by vomiting or by using laxatives. Left untreated, the disease causes vitamin deficiency and serious physical ailments such as liver, kidney, and heart disease. Repeated vomiting can rupture the stomach, and the acid in the vomit erodes tooth enamel. About 40 percent of women with bulimia develop irregular menstruation, and, like anorexics, about 20 percent stop having their periods entirely.

During the decade, theories about these disorders included psychological, biological, and social explanations. Psychological explanations for anorexia focused on the fear of maturing and the fear of loss of control. Bulimia was regarded as a fear of food that created a compulsion, which led to stress and fear around episodes of binge eating and purging. Scientists also thought the disorders might be associated with a disorder of the hypothalamus, the gland that produces hormones and regulates hunger, thirst, and temperature. Since some bulimics improved after treatment with antidepressant drugs, other scientists linked the disorder to decreased levels of the chemical serotonin in the brain. Social scientists blamed social pressures. In American society, women have been constantly bombarded with advertisements and unrealistic role models suggesting that a woman's only worth is in her youth and her slim appearances. A survey in 1984 revealed that 45 percent of underweight respondents thought they were too fat and needed to lose weight.

Residential treatment facilities for anorexics were developed during the 1980s that included family therapy and counseling. Between 15 and 25 percent of anorexics relapsed occasionally; another 15 to 20 percent continued to be anorexic. Bulimics could be treated successfully outside the hospital since their disorder was not so life threatening. Treatment usually consisted of therapy and antidepressant drugs, but a high rate of treatment failure was reported. Because anorexia nervosa and bulimia were still poorly understood, treatments for them were not universally successful in the decade.

❖ ENVIRONMENTAL MEDICINE

In the early 1980s, a new and controversial branch of medicine began to center on the links between health and environmental factors. Pollution-related health hazards were problems for decades, but the 1980s saw a growing concern about air pollution inside the home or workplace.

A major culprit was formaldehyde, a chemical preservative used in many building materials such as adhesives, furnishings, particleboard, and foam insulation. Many people suffered allergic reactions to the chemical, sometimes severely. Unfortunately, it was not the only problem. Many new homes and office buildings were made with many synthetic, chemically treated building materials and finishings. Air breathed in these buildings was contaminated by many things, including toxic carbon monoxide (from incomplete burning of fuel) and nitrogen dioxide (produced during the burning of natural gas and thought to cause increased respiratory problems in children in winter). The air in tobacco-free homes and buildings could be filled with as many as 150 contaminants from stove gases, furnaces, solvents, paints, furnishings, mold, and pesticides. Many of these chemicals occurred as ingredients or by-products of common items such as household cleansers, construction materials, and cigarettes.

New buildings were models of energy efficiency, with little outside ventilation. As a result, chemical contaminants were being trapped indoors. U.S. Environmental Protection Agency (EPA) studies of American homes

American Nobel Prize Winners in Physiology or Medicine

Year	Scientist (s)	
1980	Baruj Benacerraf	George D. Snell
1981	Roger W. Sperry	David H. Hubel
1982	No award given to an American	
1983	Barbara McClintock	
1984	No award given to an American	
1985	Michael S. Brown	Joseph L. Goldstein
1986	Stanley Cohen	Rita Levi-Montalcini
1987	No award given to an American	
1988	Gertrude B. Elion	George H. Hitchings
1989	J. Michael Bishop	Harold E. Varmus

found chemical levels that were two to five times higher indoors than outdoors. Officials estimated as many as 30 percent of new office buildings made workers ill. The EPA ranked indoor air pollution among the nation's top five environmental health problems during the decade.

Radon, a product of the radioactive breakdown of radium found in certain rock formations, also made headlines in the 1980s as people in several states found high concentrations of the radioactive gas in their homes. The colorless and odorless gas can enter a building through cracks in the foundation and can build up to potentially dangerous levels in closed areas. Long exposure to radon can lead to lung cancer. Scientists working for the Centers for Disease Control and Prevention estimated that high radon levels could cause as many as thirty thousand lung cancer deaths in the country each year. In the fall of 1985, the EPA announced plans to conduct a national survey on radon and present a five-year plan to lessen its health hazard. Pennsylvania became the first state to help home owners to measure radon levels and increase ventilation to disperse the gas.

In 1980, fewer than four of every three hundred thousand Americans died from the respiratory disease asthma. By the end of the decade, that figure had nearly doubled. No one knew for sure just why the increase occurred, but some researchers suspected outdoor and indoor air pollution. Statistics showed higher rates among minorities and city dwellers who were more likely to live and to work in "sick buildings."

Many in the medical community turned their attention to the role of the environment and to environmental medicine in the nation's public health picture. Prevention, rather than treatment, seemed to be the key. Many sick buildings in the workplace solved their air-quality problems by properly maintaining their heating, ventilation, and air-conditioning systems. Careful selection of building materials, equipment, and cleansing supplies could also limit the level of indoor contaminants.

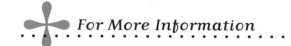 *For More Information*

BOOKS

Berger, Melvin. *The Artificial Heart.* New York: Franklin Watts, 1987.

Bianchi, Anne. *C. Everett Koop: The Health of the Nation.* Brookfield, CT: Millbrook Press, 1992.

Goodnough, David. *Eating Disorders: A Hot Issue.* Berkeley Heights: NJ: Enslow Publishers, 1999.

Mace, Nancy L., and Peter V. Rabins. *The 36-Hour Day: A Family Guide to Caring for Persons with Alzheimer's Disease, Related Dementing Illnesses, and Memory Loss in Later Life.* Third ed. Baltimore: Johns Hopkins University Press, 1999.

White, Katherine. *Everything You Need to Know About AIDS and HIV.* New York: Rosen Publishing Group, 2001.

White, Ryan, and Ann Marie Cunningham. *Ryan White: My Own Story.* New York: Dial Books, 1991.

Whitehead, Mary Beth, with Loretta Schwartz-Nobel. *A Mother's Story: The Truth About the Baby M Case.* New York: St. Martin's Press, 1989.

WEB SITES

AIDS History Center. http://www.aidshistory.org/aidshist.htm (accessed on July 29, 2002).

AIDS.ORG-Quality Treatment Information and Resources. http://www.aids.org/index.html (accessed on July 29, 2002).

Alzheimer's Disease Education and Referral (ADEAR Center). http://www.alzheimers.org/ (accessed on July 29, 2002).

CDC-NCHSTP-Divisions of HIV/AIDS Prevention (DHAP) Home Page. http://www.cdc.gov/hiv/dhap.htm (accessed on July 29, 2002).

Indoor Air Quality (IAQ). http://www.epa.gov/iaq/index.html (accessed on July 29, 2002).

National Eating Disorders Association. http://www.nationaleatingdisorders.org (accessed on July 29, 2002).

Nobel e-Museum. http://www.nobel.se/index.html (accessed on July 29, 2002).

chapter seven *Science and Technology*

1980: **January 1** Physicist Luis Alvarez proposes that the extinction of the dinosaurs occurred because of a collision of an asteroid with Earth.

1980: **February 26** The nuclear containment building at Crystal River, Florida, suffers the spillage of thousands of gallons of radioactive water.

1980: **May 18** In the state of Washington, Mount St. Helens erupts, spewing forth 51 million cubic yards of volcanic ash, dirt, and rocks, leveling nearby forests and killing sixty-two people.

1981: **April 12** NASA's first reusable spacecraft, the space shuttle *Columbia,* is successfully launched.

1981: **August 12** International Business Machines (IBM) introduces its first personal computer, with an operating system by Microsoft.

1982: **August 30** In Kenya, anthropologists report the discovery of a humanlike jawbone reportedly eight million years old.

1983: Scientists announce the apparent discovery of one of the four assumed basic forces in nature. The "W," for weak force, assumed to be the force responsible for the radioactive splitting of atoms, joins gravity, electro-

magnetism, and the strong force (which holds atomic nuclei together) as the physical constants of nature.

1983: **March 8** Apple Computer introduces a new machine, called Lisa, that features a handheld electronic pointer or "mouse."

1983: **September 14** IBM announces the development of a computer chip capable of storing 512,000 bits (512K) of information.

1984: **January 24** Apple Computer unveils its long-awaited personal computer, the Macintosh.

1984: **December 11** Astronomers at the University of Arizona at Tucson announce they have discovered the first planet outside the solar system.

1984: **December 20** A one-megabyte random access memory (RAM) chip, capable of storing four times as much information as any previous computer chip, is introduced by Bell Laboratories.

1985: English scientists report the existence of a giant "hole" in the ozone layer over Antarctica.

1985: **March 4** The U.S. Environmental Protection Agency (EPA) bans virtually all leaded gasolines in the United States.

1985: **September 1** Oceanographer and explorer Robert D. Ballard, leading a joint French-U.S. team, discovers the wreck of the *Titanic* in the Atlantic Ocean 500 miles south of Newfoundland.

1986: **January 28** The space shuttle *Challenger* explodes following liftoff in Cape Canaveral, Florida. All crew members are killed.

1986: **April 26** An accident at the Chernobyl nuclear power plant near Kiev, Ukraine, releases radioactive fallout across much of Europe and renders thousands of acres of land near the accident site uninhabitable for thousands of years.

1986: **December 23** Pilots Richard Rutan and Jeana Yeager complete the first nonstop flight around the globe on a single load of fuel in the experimental airplane *Voyager*.

1987: **March 9** Scientists testifying before the U.S. Congress announce that the ozone layer has undergone a sharp depletion in the last ten years.

1987: **April 2** IBM unveils the next generation of its personal computer.

1987: **September 16** A world environmental summit in Montreal passes measures designed to reduce the presence of ozone-depleting chlorofluorocarbons in the atmosphere.

1988: **March 14** The U.S. Senate ratifies an international agreement to phase out the use of ozone-depleting chlorofluorocarbons.

1988: **September 29** With the successful launch of the space shuttle *Discovery*, NASA resumes shuttle flights, suspended for thirty-two months following the destruction of the shuttle *Challenger* in 1986.

1989: **March 24** In the worst oil spill in American history, the oil tanker *Exxon Valdez* runs aground in Alaska, spilling almost 11 million gallons of crude oil into Prince William Sound.

1989: **June 21** Seven leading computer firms form U.S. Memories, Inc., a consortium to produce dynamic random access memory (DRAM) chips for computers.

1989: **November 19** Scientists at the California Institute of Technology announce they have discovered the oldest and most distant object yet known: a quasar at the edge of the observable universe.

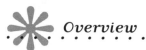

Overview

The general anxiety that many Americans felt toward science and technology in the 1970s deepened during the 1980s. The dangers of environmental pollution became more acute and expensive as thousands of hazardous waste sites were identified and the U.S. Congress moved to clean them up by establishing the Superfund. The discovery in 1985 of a hole in Earth's protective ozone layer, a hole many scientists believed was caused by man-made chemical compounds known as chlorofluorocarbons, fed concerns that technology was destroying the basic ecological foundation of human life. The 1986 nuclear disaster at Chernobyl in Ukraine, which spewed radioactive material into the atmosphere, raised further fears. The pollution-filled decade ended with a catastrophic environmental disaster, the oil spill caused by the grounding of the tanker *Exxon Valdez*.

Huge, expensive, government-sponsored science projects that paid few immediate returns and diverted resources from social programs came under attack in the decade. Public confidence in such expensive projects was deeply shaken by the explosion of the space shuttle *Challenger* shortly after its launch on January 28, 1986. For many critics, it proved the program was not worth the cost: space shuttles were expensive and complex, and their failures were far too costly.

Failure and sloppy science were not the only stories in science during the 1980s. One new technology in particular delivered the type of progressive improvement Americans had formerly associated with science: Computers had a profound impact on the decade. Capable of replicating a host of intellectual functions, computers revolutionized basic science and increased the speed and accuracy of technical applications. Moreover, when the personal computer was introduced in 1981, it began a revolution in business practices, personal finance, and communications technology whose full impact cannot yet be determined. Computers were an old-fashioned scientific success story, dramatically improving the quality of life and restoring the faith of many in the potential of technology.

Despite such great advances in technology during the decade, Americans found they could not rely on scientific methods to predict accurately the stirrings of the planet. Scientists knew that Mount St. Helens, a dormant volcano in Washington State, was becoming active in the spring of 1980, but they could not tell exactly when it would explode. And when it did, they never imagined the ferocity of the explosion once the underground forces became too great to be contained.

Luis W. Alvarez (1911–1988) In 1980, physicist Luis W. Alvarez and his son Walter proposed the theory that dinosaurs became extinct after a giant asteroid struck Earth about sixty-five million years ago. The dusty cloud thrown into the atmosphere by such a collision covered the planet for an extended period of time, blocked out sunlight, and caused the widespread death of plant life on Earth. This, in turn, brought about the extinction of plant-eating dinosaurs. While the theory has been accepted by many scientists it is still the subject of considerable debate. *Photo reproduced by permission of AP/Wide World Photos.*

Guion S. Bluford Jr. (1942–) Guion S. Bluford Jr. became the first African American to experience space flight when he served as mission specialist aboard the space shuttle *Challenger,* which launched on August 30, 1983. While in space, Bluford headed numerous scientific and technical experiments, including the release of a communications and weather satellite, tests on the shuttle's mechanical arm, and various medical experiments. He flew one more shuttle mission in the decade and two in the next before retiring from NASA. *Photo reproduced by permission of the U.S. National Aeronautics and Space Administration.*

Barbara McClintock (1902–1992) Barbara McClintock was awarded the Nobel Prize in medicine or physiology in 1983, the first woman to be the sole recipient of a Nobel Prize in that field. In the early 1950s, while studying the structure of Indian corn, she found that genetic material could shift unpredictably from one generation to the next. McClintock's discovery of mobile or "jumping" genes went against established theories of genetics. However, it took the scientific community more than thirty years to acknowledge she had made one of the most fundamental discoveries in the field of genetics in the twentieth century. *Photo reproduced by permission of AP/Wide World Photos.*

Sally Ride (1951–) Sally Ride became the first American woman in space when she was chosen as one of the crew members of the space shuttle *Challenger.* The seventh space shuttle fight, it lifted off on June 18, 1983. While in space, Ride helped deploy two communications satellites, conducted trials of the mechanical arm she had helped design, and performed and monitored about forty scientific experiments. She flew on her second, and final, shuttle mission the following year. In 1986, she served as the only astronaut on the presidential commission investigating the *Challenger* explosion. *Photo reproduced by permission of AP/Wide World Photos.*

Topics in the News • • • • • • • • • • • • • • • • • • •

❖ NASA SPACE SHUTTLES: TRIUMPH TO DISASTER

The National Aeronautics and Space Administration (NASA), a civilian government agency, witnessed both great triumph and immense disaster in the 1980s. With the creation of the Space Transportation System (STS), more commonly referred to as the space shuttle, NASA fundamentally shifted its approach to space travel. The space shuttle was to replace traditional expendable launch vehicles as it was to be the first in the line of reusable spaceships. Competition in the race for space had increased in recent years, as both Europe and the Soviet Union had found more-economical methods of exploration. An organization that had long been underfunded by the federal government, NASA was searching for a new symbol to retain its prestige as the premier space exploration organization in the world. With the shuttle in operation, all appeared to be in order.

On April 12, 1981, NASA launched the space shuttle *Columbia*, which was to be the first in a long line of reusable, cost-efficient spacecraft. The shuttles were multifunctional vehicles designed to provide reliable and consistent travel into space. Their winged shape was similar to that of airplanes, yet the 184-foot-long vessels could carry with them up to seven passengers and several satellites. Its cargo bay was 15 feet wide and 60 feet long and it could haul payloads up to 65,000 pounds. Space shuttles were launched with the aid of two solid booster rockets and an external tank, expendable pieces that separated from the shuttle once it had cleared Earth's atmosphere. NASA touted the craft as being able to perform dozens of missions a year with minimal repair. The shuttle was unable to perform under the vigorous standards that were set for it, however, and as a result, NASA frequently cut corners and sacrificed safety to meet its goals.

Despite problems with the program, the shuttle accomplished a string of historic successes, one of which was the fifth shuttle flight on November 11, 1982, the first operational mission, which launched two communication satellites. Sally K. Ride made history on June 18, 1983, when she became the United States' first woman astronaut in space. Other memorable flights included those in which members of the U.S. Congress rode on board and flights in which commercial satellites were released, retrieved, or repaired in space. NASA intended to have a team of shuttles constantly in action; yet its schedule was severely obstructed by technical, financial, and weather constraints.

After twenty-four successful missions, NASA and the country had come to view space shuttle launches as routine, but the launch of the space shuttle *Challenger* on January 28, 1986, changed those perceptions forever. During its six-day mission, in addition to the usual scientific experiments and satellite release and retrieval that had marked almost all previous shuttle missions, *Challenger* was to feature live broadcasts to the nation's schoolchildren by high-school social studies teacher Sharon Christa McAuliffe. As part of the Teacher in Space Project, McAuliffe had been chosen from among the nation's teachers to become the first ordinary American to travel aboard a space shuttle. She was to have taught two lessons from space. Joining McAuliffe on the *Challenger* were pilot Michael J. Smith, flight commander Francis R. Scobee, physicist Ronald E. McNair, electrical engineer Judith A. Resnik, aeronautical engineer Ellison S. Onizuka, and electrical engineer Gregory B. Jarvis.

About 59 seconds into the launch, a plume of fire flamed out of the right-hand booster rocket, jetting down toward the giant fuel tank. By 64 seconds into launch, the fire burned a gaping hole in the casing of the booster. At 72 seconds, it loosened the strut that attached the booster to the external tank. One second later, the loosened booster rocket slammed into the tip of *Challenger*'s right wing. Then, at 74 seconds into the launch, at an altitude of 46,000 feet, the booster rocket crashed into the fuel tank and set off a massive explosion. The shuttle was traveling about twice the speed of sound, almost 1,500 miles per hour.

Challenger exploded 20 miles off the coast of Florida. The force of the explosion sent debris 20 miles above Earth. Burning fragments of the shuttle rained down on recovery operations for the next hour. The seven-person crew was inside a module that detached from the shuttle during the explosion. Evidence collected later indicated that the crew members survived the explosion, only to die when their craft slammed into the Atlantic Ocean at a speed of nearly 2,000 miles per hour after a 9-mile free fall. It is unknown if the entire crew remained conscious throughout the 2-minute fall, but at least two crew members activated emergency air packs.

Of all the accidents in the twenty-five-year history of manned spaceflight, the *Challenger* disaster was by far the worst. The disaster, viewed continuously on television, sent shock waves through the nation. President Ronald Reagan (1911–) established a presidential commission to investigate the accident, and it released its findings in June 1986. The Rogers Commission, chaired by William B. Rogers, the former secretary of state, identified two primary reasons for the shuttle's destruction. The first lay in the faulty design of the craft's rubber O-rings, the seals used to join sections of the two solid-rocket boosters on either side of the shuttle. The rings' function was to keep certain gases from escaping by expanding to fill the gaps. They were sensitive to temperature shifts, and their designer,

Morton Thiokol, and NASA were both familiar with the fact that the rings had sometimes failed to expand properly on previous shuttle flights. Their mistake was underestimating the importance of the problem. The second major flaw the commission named was the fact that the *Challenger* was

The Chernobyl Disaster

Thousands of miles away from America's shores, the events of April 26, 1986, focused concern on the issue of safety in the nuclear power industry. One of four nuclear reactors at the Chernobyl Nuclear Power Plant near Kiev in Ukraine exploded with such force that the roof of the building was completely blown off. Eight tons of radioactive material was scattered about the region immediately surrounding the plant. Airborne radioactivity from the blast rained down on northern Europe and Scandinavia (fallout was measured as far away as Scotland), contaminating farm produce.

Engineers at Chernobyl had accidentally initiated an uncontrolled chain reaction in the reactor's core during an unauthorized test in which they unlawfully disabled the reactor's emergency systems. In the immediate aftermath of the catastrophe, more than thirty people lost their lives. More than a decade later, the remains of the Chernobyl reactor were still far too radioactive for anyone to spend more than a few minutes in the area. Scientists estimate that the lives of some twenty thousand people will be shortened as a result of the effects of exposure to radiation from the accident.

launched at a much colder temperature than any other previous launch. In the frigid temperatures that day, the O-rings became less flexible than normal, and they failed to seal the joints completely.

Other discoveries of the commission shed a harsh light on NASA, suggesting that it was an organization riddled with incompetence and a top-heavy management structure that did not allow critical information to reach the right people. The House Science and Technology Committee concurred with the Rogers Commission's finding, which blamed NASA for setting unrealistic goals to be met in such short periods of time that safety was compromised. On August 15, 1986, President Reagan commissioned NASA to begin construction of a new shuttle and to make safety issues a primary concern.

The space shuttle program was grounded for more than two years, and NASA worked to rebuild its credibility and the nation's confidence in space travel. The twenty-sixth space shuttle mission did not leave the launchpad until September 29, 1988. To everyone's relief, *Discovery* lifted off without incident that day. *Endeavour,* the shuttle built to replace *Challenger,* first flew on May 7, 1992.

During the 1980s, the people of the United States lived a life of comfort never before seen in human history for so large and diverse a people. The country's comparative affluence had, however, a major side effect: pollution. While producing an extensive amount of goods for the market, the nation had also been pouring vast quantities of pollutants into the soil, water, and air.

For decades, chemicals and other toxic materials had been disposed of inappropriately across the nation. To correct this and the growing pollution problem, the U.S. Congress established the Superfund in 1980 to clean up toxic waste dumps across America. The Superfund provided three essential things in the fight against toxic waste sites: it put the federal government in charge of identifying public sites; it provided for fines to be levied on chemical manufacturers to assist in funding the cleanup; and it held companies that had contributed to a toxic site accountable, however large or small their contribution.

The new act initially provided more than $1 billion for a Hazardous Substance Response Trust Fund. It soon became clear that even this amount might not be enough to clean up the tons of toxic chemicals buried and abandoned in sites scattered all across the country. During the decade, only twenty-seven sites had been cleaned so thoroughly that they were removed from the Superfund list of hazardous sites. Although by 1989 the federal Superfund had over $8 billion for cleanup of toxic sites, well over a thousand sites remained on the inventory list of those in need of cleanup.

❖ THE GROWING OZONE PROBLEM

When three atoms of oxygen bond, they form a molecule of ozone (O_3). Ozone is both much rarer and much more chemically active than atmospheric oxygen (O_2), the common form of oxygen found on Earth. Nevertheless, ozone posed two significant health risks during the 1980s. The first problem was there was too much of it in urban areas near the planet's surface. The second problem was there was not enough of it at high altitudes. Both problems were manmade.

Ozone is a classic example of a chemical that is both helpful and harmful. Most of the ozone in Earth's atmosphere is located within the

Exxon Valdez

When the *Exxon Valdez* ran aground on a charted reef in Prince William Sound in Alaska shortly after midnight on March 24, 1989, it spilled almost eleven million gallons of crude oil into the pristine waters and smeared black goo across an estimated 1,300 miles of coastline. It was the worst oil spill in American history.

Completed in 1986, the *Exxon Valdez* was the largest ship ever built on the west coast of the United States. It measured 987 feet long, 166 feet wide, and 88 feet deep from its main deck to its flat keel. When fully loaded, it could transport more than 62 million gallons of crude oil.

Piloting the tanker that night was the third mate, who was overly tired and suffering under a heavy workload. The captain, Joseph Hazelwood, was useless in providing a proper navigation watch. Tests subsequently revealed he had been drinking before the tanker ran aground. He was later found not guilty of operating the tanker while under the influence of alcohol. Hazelwood was eventually convicted of only one charge: negligent discharge of oil. That verdict was later overturned on appeal.

stratosphere (second atmospheric layer above ground level) between nine and eighteen miles above Earth's surface. Temperatures above the ozone layer, or ozonosphere, are warmer because ozone molecules absorb the Sun's ultraviolet radiation (energy in the form of waves or particles) and transform it into heat energy. Ozone in the atmosphere at this level is critically important because it prevents ultraviolet light and other harmful radiation from reaching the surface of the planet. Ultraviolet radiation is known to affect the growth of certain kinds of plants, to cause eye damage in animals, to disrupt the function of DNA (the genetic material in an organism), and to cause skin cancer in humans.

Ozone in the troposphere, the atmospheric layer closest to Earth's surface, is harmful, even deadly. The primary sources of ozone in the air humans breathe are gases released from the tailpipes of automobiles and the smokestacks of factories. In the presence of sunlight, these gases can react with atmospheric oxygen to form ozone, which has harmful effects on both plants and animals. Ozone seriously injures the leaves of most

The effect of the spill on the environment was immediate and devastating. Scientists estimated that 250,000 seabirds, 2,800 sea otters, 300 harbor seals, 250 bald eagles, and as many as 22 orcas were killed by the spill. Countless other animals perished as well. Oil drifted as far west as the Aleutian Peninsula. Cleanup efforts began immediately and lasted for over four years. At the peak of the effort, ten thousand workers, one thousand ships, one hundred aircraft, and numerous federal agencies were involved. It is widely believed, however, that wave action from winter storms did more to clean the beaches than all the human effort involved.

The Exxon Corporation, the tanker's owner, spent more than $2 billion on the cleanup effort. It spent another $1 billion to settle civil and criminal charges related to the case. The commercial fishing industry and the tourist industry in the area suffered an untold loss. Ten years after the spill, many fish and wildlife species had not fully recovered. Some scientists believe the amount of damage caused by the spill may never be known and some species may never recover.

plants, reducing their ability to photosynthesize (photosynthesis is a complicated process in which plants utilize light energy to form carbohydrates and release oxygen as a by-product). In humans and other animals, the gas irritates and damages membranes of the respiratory system and eyes. It can also induce asthma.

In the 1980s, in many areas where automotive exhaust and industries were concentrated, the problem of ozone in the air near ground level was often very serious. In 1987, Los Angeles's ozone levels exceeded federal health standards on 141 days. The problem extended nationwide. That same year, ozone levels exceeded federal standards on nineteen days in New York City, on twenty-one days in Houston, and on twenty-three days in Philadelphia.

While ozone was accumulating in the lower atmosphere, scientists found it was being destroyed in the ozonosphere. In 1985, English scientists first reported that the ozone layer above Antarctica appeared to be thinning. In fact, the amount had dropped to such a low level that the term "hole" was used to describe the condition. In succeeding years, the hole reappeared with the onset of each summer season in Antarctica (September through December). The potential threat to human and other life forms on the planet was obvious to many scientists.

Scientists soon presented evidence that a group of chemical compounds known as chlorofluorocarbons (CFCs) might be causing the destruction of the ozone layer. CFCs had been created in 1928 for use as a refrigerant. Over the years, they became widely popular for use as propellants in aerosol sprays, as blowing agents in the manufacture of plastic foams and insulation, as dry-cleaning fluids, and as cleaning agents for electronic components, among other applications. In 1978, the U.S. Food and Drug Administration (FDA) banned CFCs in aerosol products in the United States, but problems persisted.

A movement arose to reduce or ban the use of these chemical compounds. In 1987, in a conference sponsored by the United Nations Environment Programme, many countries signed the so-called Montreal Proto-

Data from the Total Ozone Mapping Spectrometer (TOPS) Earth Probe. Areas of depleted ozone over the Antarctic can be seen as a haze. Reproduced by permission of AP/Wide World Photos.

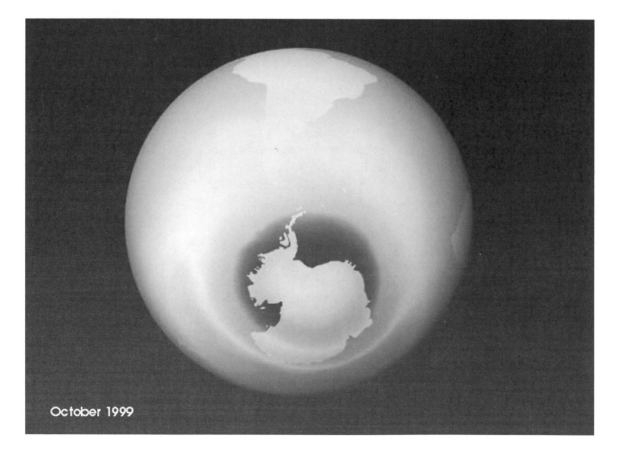

October 1999

col, which set specific time limits for the phasing out of both the production and use of CFCs. Despite these steps, and others taken afterward, scientists were not optimistic. CFCs already released into the atmosphere will continue to destroy the ozone layer for another century. Some scientists predicted that as many as eight hundred thousand people could die from the ill effects caused by the additional ultraviolet radiation that will reach Earth's surface during those years.

❖ THE COMPUTER REVOLUTION

By the mid-1980s, computer technology had transformed American life. The watches people wore, the cars they drove, the mail they received, the games they played, the state of their health, and the way they learned were altered by the computer chip. Schools, workplaces, the health industry, government, and the law were all dramatically affected by the computer.

Big businesses had long recognized the importance of the computer. By the 1980s, however, as computer equipment and the programs to make it useful became affordable, even small business offices relied on computers for word processing, accounting, record keeping, and a variety of specialized uses limited only by the imagination of programmers. Computers changed the way telephone systems operated and were managed. Banking moved swiftly from personal service to computerized automatic teller machines (ATMs). Computer-driven robots reshaped manufacturing processes. Computer-assisted teleconferencing began to be recognized as an efficient alternative to expensive business travel. Even show business was affected as computerized synthesizers were developed that could emulate the sound of any musical instrument, and filmmakers used computers to design and execute special effects.

Of equal, if not greater, importance was the personal computer revolution that decade. What the average American commonly refers to as a PC, or personal computer, did not even exist before the 1970s. Room-sized mainframe computers had been the norm, and they were primarily relegated to business and scientific use. With the dawn of the personal computer, all Americans were allowed potential access to computers. Companies such as Apple Computer became household names, and words such as software and downloading became commonplace. It was predicted that by 1990, 60 percent of all the jobs in the United States would require familiarity with computers. Already by 1985, some two million Americans were using personal computers to perform various tasks in the office.

Apple Computer, founded in 1976 by Steven Jobs and Stephen Wozniak, spearheaded the personal computer revolution, developing its innova-

Machine of the Year

At the beginning of every year, *Time* magazine publishes a Man of the Year issue in which it bestows that title on a single person (man or woman) who made a significant mark, for better or worse, on the world in the preceding year. In January 1983, the editors of the magazine named the personal computer its 1982 Machine of the Year, solidifying the arrival of the PC into mainstream American society. Some critics scoffed at the fact the magazine had bestowed such an important title on a machine, but the editors of *Time* defended their position. By adapting the honor for a machine, *Time* acknowledged the immense contribution the PC had made upon society. Computers, once available only to trained programmers, had become increasingly commonplace in homes across the country. They completely changed the way average Americans received and processed information at work and at home, and they would continue to do so for years to come.

tive vision of how computers could relate to the average person. In 1983, Apple introduced the Lisa, the first computer to introduce the concept of windows, menus, icons, and a mouse to the mainstream. The Lisa computer was phased out by 1985 and surpassed by the Macintosh in 1984. The Macintosh was faster, smaller, and less costly than the Lisa. Packaged as a user-friendly machine that was economical enough to be in every home, the Macintosh did not require its user to have programming knowledge in order to operate it, and it became popular.

In 1986, Apple introduced the Mac Plus computer, and the Laserwriter printer. The introduction of these two, along with Adobe PageMaker, an easy-to-use graphics page-layout program, helped give rise to a new medium known as desktop publishing. Creating this new niche made Macintosh the premier, efficient publishing computer. Apple expanded its hold on the graphics market in 1987 with the introduction of the Mac II computer. Its color graphic capability encouraged the creation of color printers capable of reproducing the color images on the computer screen.

Despite Apple's successes, International Business Machines (IBM) remained the largest computer firm in the world. In August 1981, IBM had introduced its first personal computer. Simply called the IBM PC, it became the definition for the personal computer. IBM was the largest of the three giant computer firms in the world, and the other two, Hewlett-Packard and Xerox, had previously attempted to make efforts into the new PC market but failed. IBM initially was not convinced that the American public was interested in computers, particularly for home usage, but after viewing the early successes of Apple, they were determined to enter the race. To create software for the PC, IBM turned in 1981 to a young company called Microsoft to formulate the computer operating system which became known as MS-DOS (Microsoft Disk Operating System).

IBM PCs were immensely powerful, fast machines for their time, and their entrance into the market legitimized the personal computer and created a new industry. By the mid-1980s, IBM PCs had inspired other companies to produce "IBM clones" that copied IBM's hardware and software at a lower cost to consumers. Constantly setting the standard, IBM established agreements with software companies such as Lotus to develop sophisticated programming. Even with several marketing setbacks throughout the decade, IBM managed to remain on top of the growing computer world. By 1989, IBM was producing personal computers that dwarfed earlier models in speed, capability, and technology.

As the personal computer world continued to grow, it spawned other industries. One of the largest new markets to develop was that of the software industry, and one of the largest companies in that industry was Microsoft, founded in 1975 by Bill Gates and Paul Allen in Redmond, Washington. Microsoft's MS-DOS, initially licensed only to IBM, became the industry-standard operating software for all PCs by the end of the decade. The ability to corner the fast-growing software market solidified Microsoft's leadership position in the 1980s. Late in the decade, Microsoft also began work on the Windows software program for PCs and introduced programs for Apple Computer.

Bill Gates, founder and CEO of Microsoft.
Reproduced by permission of the Microsoft Corporation.

❖ MOUNT ST. HELENS

Located seventy miles from Portland, Oregon, in a sparsely populated region of southwestern Washington state in the Cascade mountain range,

Mount St. Helens erupted in 1980 in one of the largest volcanic explosions in North American history. The blast was equivalent in power to the largest hydrogen bomb ever exploded. The volcano's last eruption had been recorded by the American explorer and army officer John C. Frémont (1813–1890) in 1857.

After having lain dormant since the mid-nineteenth century, Mount St. Helens came alive in March 1980. In the two months before the eruption, Mount St. Helens experienced more than ten thousand small earthquakes and hundreds of small eruptions involving blasts of steam. Also during that time, the north slope of the volcano bulged outward more than 260 feet. On March 27, there was an explosion that created a 200-foot hole in the mountainside. The next day a plume of steam, ash, and gas erupted from the volcano and rose 4 miles into the atmosphere.

A 1980 eruption of Mount St. Helens in Skamania, Washington. **Reproduced by permission of the Corbis Corporation.**

Sensing an impending eruption, scientists advised as many as 250,000 residents in nearby counties, including several hundred loggers, forest rangers, and residents in the immediate vicinity of Mount St. Helens, to leave the area. Roadblocks were set up around the perimeter of the volcano,

although a number of people such as backpackers and loggers continued to slip through. The United States Geological Survey (USGS) assigned a scientific team of twenty-four volcano-watchers to monitor the volcano.

The quiet dawn of May 18, 1980, was shattered when an earthquake measuring 5.1 on the Richter scale rumbled beneath the volcano at 8:27 A.M., weakening its crater rim. Four minutes later, the north face of the volcano collapsed and slid downward in the largest landslide in recorded history. As the cone crumbled, gas was released and the magma was exposed. At 8:32 A.M., the volcano exploded in a blast that was heard as far away as Vancouver, Canada, some 200 miles to the north. Instead of moving straight upward, the hot gas, steam, ash, and rock fragments the volcano spewed forth traveled sideways to the north where the crater rim had been destroyed. The flow of hot ash and gas raced across the ground at speeds approaching 80 miles per hour. At a temperature of at least 1,300 degrees Fahrenheit, it burned everything it touched for an area of 6 square miles. The flying debris, gas, and heat killed millions of wildlife including deer, elk, coyotes, bobcats, black beers, mountain lions, birds, and other animals. The windstorm produced by the eruption was powerful enough to flatten trees and to pick up and toss around logging trucks and bulldozers several miles from the volcano.

The heat from the eruption melted snow and ice on the volcano. This water combined with ash and chunks of ice to form mudflows that filled riverbeds and lakes, and buried houses, roads, and bridges. Millions of trout and salmon died in the mud-choked rivers. The flow of the Columbia River, a main thoroughfare to the Pacific Ocean, was blocked by mud.

The eruption sent a cloud containing millions of tons of dust and ash fifteen miles into the air. As the cloud spread across 22,000 miles of western U.S. skies, the Sun was blocked out. Residents of Spokane, Washington, 250 miles from Mount St. Helens, experienced complete darkness throughout the day of the eruption. Crops in parts of Washington, Oregon, and Idaho were blanketed by ash that fell to the ground in the days after the eruption. The cloud spread across the country in three days and circled the planet in fifteen days.

Sixty-two people lost their lives in the eruption of Mount St. Helens. Most of the victims choked to death on volcanic ash. People located eighteen miles north of the volcano were killed by heat, ash, showering rocks, and lethal gases in the eruption. Prior to the blast, scientists had determined that 16 miles from the volcano would be a safe distance. They never imagined the volcano would spew its stream sideways.

Before May 18, Mount St. Helens had stood at 9,677 feet. The fifth-tallest peak in Washington, it was also one of the most picturesque, its nearly per-

American Nobel Prize Winners in Chemistry or Physics

Year	Scientist(s)	Field
1980	Paul Berg Walter Gilbert	Chemistry
	James Watson Cronin Val Logsdon Fitch	Physics
1981	Roald Hoffmann	Chemistry
	Nicolaas Bloembergen Arthur Leonard Schawlow	Physics
1982	Kenneth G. Wilson	Physics
1983	Henry Taube	Chemistry
	Subramanyan Chandrasekhar William Alfred Fowler	Physics
1984	Robert Bruce Merrifield	Chemistry
1985	Herbert A. Hauptman Jerome Karle	Chemistry
1986	Dudley R. Herschbach Yuan T. Lee	Chemistry
1987	Donald J. Cram Charles J. Pederson	Chemistry
1988	Leon M. Lederman Melvin Schwartz Jack Steinberger	Physics
1989	Sidney Altman Thomas R. Cech	Chemistry
	Norman F. Ramsey Hans G. Dehmelt	Physics

fect cone shape capped by snow and ice. The eruption removed the uppermost 1,314 feet of the mountain, dropping it to the fifteenth-tallest peak in the state. The crater and north side of the mountain, including the crater rim, were destroyed, leaving the crater clearly visible after the eruption.

Despite the incredible destruction to the surrounding landscape, plants began to reappear in the area just a few months after the eruption, and, slowly, wildlife returned to the region. Volcanic activity, however, continued. A second eruption occurred on May 25, a week after the initial blast. A dome of molten rock had formed by October 1980, and another, less spectacular, eruption took place on April 11, 1981. Five years later, in May and June 1985, a series of minor earthquakes accompanied by mild volcanic activity worried residents, but no major volcanic activity followed. Although they cannot accurately predict when, scientists believe the volcano may erupt again early in the twenty-first century.

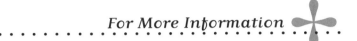

For More Information

BOOKS

Burgess, Colin. *Teacher in Space: Christa McAuliffe and the Challenger Legacy.* Lincoln: University of Nebraska Press, 2000.

Carson, Rob. *Mount St. Helens: The Eruption and Recovery of a Volcano.* Seattle, WA: Sasquatch Books, 2000.

Cheney, Glenn Alan. *Chernobyl: The Ongoing Story of the World's Deadliest Nuclear Disaster.* New York: New Discovery Books, 1993.

Dils, Tracy E. *The Exxon Valdez.* Philadelphia, PA: Chelsea House, 2001.

Freiberger, Paul, and Michael Swaine. *Fire in the Valley: The Making of the Personal Computer.* Collector's ed. New York: McGraw-Hill, 1999.

Morgan, Sally. *Ozone Hole.* New York: Franklin Watts, 1999.

WEB SITES

Challenger, STS-51L Information. http://www.hq.nasa.gov/office/pao/History/sts51l.html (accessed on July 29, 2002).

CVO Menu-Mount St. Helens, Washington. http://vulcan.wr.usgs.gov/Volcanoes/MSH/framework.html (accessed on July 29, 2002).

Mount St. Helens. http://volcano.und.nodak.edu/vwdocs/msh/msh.html (accessed on July 29, 2002).

NASA Human SpaceFlight. http://spaceflight.nasa.gov/ (accessed on July 29, 2002).

Nobel e-Museum. http://www.nobel.se/index.html (accessed on July 29, 2002).

U.S. EPA: Ozone Depletion. http://www.epa.gov/docs/ozone/index.html (accessed on July 29, 2002).

chapter eight **Sports**

1980: **February 12 to 24** The Winter Olympics are held in Lake Placid, New York.

1980: **June 6** Nineteen-year-old Wayne Gretzky of the Edmonton Oilers becomes the youngest player ever to win two major NHL awards in the same season.

1980: **July 19 to August 3** The Summer Olympics are held in Moscow, the first games ever staged in a communist nation.

1981: **March 29** Phil Mahre becomes the first American to win the men's overall World Cup skiing championship.

1981: **April 9** Frank Robinson of the San Francisco Giants becomes the first African American manager in the National League.

1981: **July 31** A forty-nine-day strike by baseball players, the longest in the history of professional sports, ends.

1982: **May 16** The New York Islanders sweep the Vancouver Canucks to become the first U.S.-based NHL team to win three consecutive Stanley Cups.

1982: **June 8** Wayne Gretzky of the Edmonton Oilers becomes the first player to

win an NHL MVP award by a unanimous vote.

1982: **November 17** A fifty-seven-day strike by NFL players ends.

1983: **July 2** Martina Navratilova wins her fourth women's singles tennis championship at Wimbledon.

1983: **September 26** *Australia II* beats the U.S. yacht *Liberty* to win the America's Cup, the first American loss in the 132-year history of the yachting competition.

1983: **November 16** Cal Ripken Jr. becomes the first player in baseball history to win Rookie of the Year and MVP awards in consecutive seasons.

1984: **February 8 to 19** The Winter Olympics are held in Sarajevo, Yugoslavia.

1984: **May 15** Magic Johnson of the Los Angeles Lakers sets an NBA playoff-game record by passing for twenty-four assists.

1984: **July 28 to August 12** The Summer Olympics are held in Los Angeles, California.

1985: **February 6** Diann Roffe becomes the first American woman to win a gold medal at the World Alpine Skiing Championship.

1985: March 6 Heavyweight Mike Tyson knocks out Hector Mercedes in the first round to win his first professional fight.

1985: May 16 Michael Jordan of the Chicago Bulls is named the NBA Rookie of the Year.

1986: May 28 Larry Bird wins his third consecutive NBA MVP award.

1986: July 23 Greg LeMond wins professional cycling's prestigious Tour de France, the first American to do so.

1986: November 22 Mike Tyson knocks out WBC champion Trevor Berbick in the second round to become, at twenty, the youngest heavyweight champion in history.

1987: April 9 Wayne Gretzky of the Edmonton Oilers breaks the all-time NHL playoff scoring mark of 176 points set by Jean Beliveau.

1987: May 30 Guard Isiah Thomas of the Detroit Pistons says that if Larry Bird of the Boston Celtics were black instead of white, he would be considered "just another good guy."

1987: December 6 San Francisco 49ers quarterback Joe Montana completes an NFL record twenty-two straight passes against the Green Bay Packers.

1988: February 13 to 28 The Winter Olympics are held in Calgary, Canada.

1988: September 17 to October 2 The Summer Olympics are held in Seoul, South Korea.

1988: September 29 Sisters-in-law Jackie Joyner-Kersee and Florence Griffith Joyner both win gold medals and set world records in their respective Olympic events: Joyner-Kersee in the heptathlon and Griffith Joyner in the 200-meter dash.

1989: July 23 Greg LeMond wins cycling's Tour de France for the second time.

1989: August 24 Cincinnati Reds manager Pete Rose agrees to a lifetime suspension from baseball for gambling.

1989: October 3 Art Shell is hired as the coach of the Los Angeles Raiders, becoming the first African American NFL coach since Fritz Pollard served as player-coach for the Hammond (Indiana) Pros (1923–25).

✳ *Overview*

The trio of major American professional sports—baseball, basketball, football—were marked in the 1980s by labor disputes, lawsuits, and rising salaries, much as they had been in the previous decade. Although many sports fans were annoyed by such problems, they did not stay away from the stadiums and fields. Throughout the 1980s, American sports enjoyed unprecedented financial prosperity and mass popularity.

Baseball still captured the nation's summertime attention. By the end of the decade, over fifty million fans annually attended major-league games and baseball's revenues were more than $1 billion a year. For baseball in the 1980s, it was both the best of times and the worst of times. Despite being a lucrative industry, it suffered terribly from bitter labor conflicts. The most pressing concern remained the power struggle between team owners and the union representing major-league baseball players.

The American public had all but given up on professional basketball at the end of the 1970s. Then came the arrival of two young players fresh out of college, one black and one white, who transformed the game forever. Earvin "Magic" Johnson and Larry Bird dueled throughout the decade, challenging each other to rise to ever greater athletic heights. In the process, they raised standards for the rest of the players as well. By the end of the decade, basketball was thriving in America. It would continue to do so in the next decade, led by the high-flying exploits of the league's 1985 Rookie of the Year: Michael Jordan.

Marred by two strikes and the movement of teams from one city to another, professional football was saved only by the accomplishments of the players on the field. Responsible for many of the decade's best moments on the gridiron was Joe Montana of the San Francisco 49ers. Many consider him the greatest quarterback the game has ever seen. Neither big nor fast, Montana was fluid and always in control. With steely determination, he had the ability to impose a quiet order on a raw and disorderly game, leading his team time after time to victory in the final moments of play.

The decade witnessed the return of legends and the birth of new ones in other American sports. Jack Nicklaus, who had dominated the game of golf for nearly two decades, was forty years old when the 1980s began, and many thought his time had passed. Nicklaus proved them wrong, continuing to display the shots and mental toughness that had made him a legend in the first place. Professional hockey welcomed a teenager who, over the course of the decade, would distance himself from virtually everyone in the sport. Never the fastest or strongest player on his team, Wayne Gretzky was far from ordinary, dominating the flow and pace of the game like no one before.

The achievement of athletes in various sports shone in the 1980s. John McEnroe ruled over professional tennis in the first half of the decade with his graceful shots and often coarse behavior. In 1986, Greg LeMond became the first American to win the Tour de France, the world's greatest cycling race. And in the Olympics, the incredible feats of the 1980 U.S. men's hockey team, speed skater Eric Heiden, and track star Carl Lewis captured the imagination of the American public. No less amazing were the victories of female athletes at the Games. Speed skater Bonnie Blair, gymnast Mary Lou Retton, and track-and-field stars Florence Griffith Joyner and Jackie Joyner-Kersee destroyed ancient myths about female athletic inferiority, providing young women in America and around the world with important role models.

Larry Bird (1957–) Larry Bird helped revive professional basketball in America. In 1980, his rookie season, he helped the Boston Celtics win thirty-two more games than they won the previous season. For his effort, he won Rookie of the Year honors. The following season, he led the Celtics to the first of three NBA championships the team would win in the 1980s. In two of those championship games, 1985 and 1986, he was named MVP. For three consecutive seasons, from 1984 to 1986, Bird was voted the league's MVP. *Photo reproduced by permission of the Corbis Corporation.*

Wayne Gretzky (1961–) Wayne Gretzky dominated professional hockey as no other individual dominated his or her sport in the 1980s. From 1980 to 1988, he scored 583 goals and handed out 1,086 assists. For six of those years, he averaged 73 goals and 130 assists a season; no one else in the history of the NHL had managed to score 200 points in a season. He won eight MVP awards and led the Edmonton Oilers to four Stanley Cup championships. In 1989, he broke the NHL's all-time scoring record of 1,850 points and won the MVP award yet again. *Photo reproduced by permission of the Corbis Corporation.*

Earvin "Magic" Johnson (1958–) Earvin "Magic" Johnson helped make professional basketball the most popular sport in the United States in the 1980s. His relentless passion for the game made him one of the most popular players in basketball. Johnson had a great scoring touch, superb ball-handling skills, and the ability always to find an open teammate with a bullet pass. He led the Los Angeles Lakers to eight of the decade's ten NBA championship games, helping the team win five of those games. In 1987, he won both the regular season and the finals MVP awards. *Photo reproduced by permission of the Corbis Corporation.*

Michael Jordan (1963–) Michael Jordan became one of the highest-paid and certainly one of the best-known athletes in the history of organized sports after he became a professional basketball player in 1984. He quickly set the standard for athletic creativity and earned a special place in basketball history. In his third season as a professional, Jordan scored over three thousand points, only the second player in NBA history to reach that mark. The intensely competitive guard for the Chicago Bulls dominated professional basketball—offensively, defensively, and aesthetically—during the latter part of the 1980s and into the 1990s. *Photo reproduced by permission of the Corbis Corporation.*

Jackie Joyner-Kersee (1962–) Jackie Joyner-Kersee has been described as the greatest multi-event track and field athlete of all time and the world's greatest female athlete. A participant in both the 1984 and 1988 Summer Olympics, Joyner-Kersee became the first American woman ever to win a gold medal in the long jump and the first woman in history to earn more than seven thousand points in the grueling seven-event heptathlon. Between her Olympic appearances, she won each of the nine heptathlons she entered and made the world record in that event her personal domain. *Photo reproduced by permission of AP/Wide World Photos.*

Joe Montana (1956–) Quarterback Joe Montana led the San Francisco 49ers to four Super Bowl titles in four appearances (1982, 1985, 1989, and 1990), and he became the only player to be awarded the championship game's MVP trophy three times. In those four bowl games, he completing 83 of 122 passes (68 percent) for 1,142 yards with 11 touchdowns and no interceptions. Montana's true worth as a quarterback lay in his ability to bring his team back from the edge of defeat in the final minutes of play, an ability perhaps unmatched in the history of the NFL. *Photo reproduced by permission of the Corbis Corporation.*

Martina Navratilova (1956–) Martina Navratilova redefined the game of women's tennis. Noted for her remarkable speed, strength, and power (her left-handed first serve was timed at 93 miles per hour), Navratilova brought an attack mentality to the sport. Throughout much of the decade, other players on the tour were unable to keep up with her serve-and-volley style of play. From 1982 to 1986, she was the top-ranked women's tennis player. By the time Navratilova retired in 1993, she had won 167 tournament titles and 55 Gland Slam titles, more than any other male or female professional tennis player. *Photo reproduced by permission of AP/Wide World Photos.*

Mike Tyson (1966–) In 1986, Mike Tyson became the youngest heavyweight world champion in history. He captivated the imagination of the public in a way no prizefighter had since Muhammad Ali. Tyson was known primarily for his powerful punching ability, his gladiatorlike temperament, and his aura of invincibility. Unbeaten as a professional in the 1980s, Tyson completely dominated his weight division: all but four of his thirty-six fights ended in knockouts. By the end of the 1980s, however, his personal life began to spin out of control, and it would fall apart in the next decade. *Photo reproduced by permission of the Corbis Corporation.*

 *Topics in the News*

❖ BASEBALL: STILL AMERICA'S PASTIME

Perhaps the best thing that can be said about major league baseball in the 1980s is that it survived. Although the decade witnessed superb individual and team performances on the field, professional baseball was probably more noted for its labor disputes, strikes, threats of strikes, owner-collusion scandals, many substance-abuse revelations, and allegations of gambling by players. But despite these and other serious problems, baseball somehow remained vibrant and popular.

In 1980, for instance, a record forty-three million people paid to see major league baseball games, income from baseball television contracts accounted for a record 30 percent of the game's $500-million revenue, and television ratings for the World Series had never been higher. Over the course of the decade, all of these leading indicators continued to improve. Contrary to the claims of some critics, baseball's place as the national pastime did not diminish.

Several teams won more than one pennant in the 1980s: The St. Louis Cardinals won three, while the Kansas City Royals, Los Angeles Dodgers, Oakland Athletics, and Philadelphia Phillies won two apiece. No team, however, was able to win the World Series back-to-back. Some observers suggested that the ability of players to become free agents, signing with teams willing to pay their high salaries, contributed to the equality among the teams. Others believed the expansion of major league clubs helped even out competition. No matter what the reasons were, the decline of baseball dynasties clearly did not hinder the game. In fact, it probably contributed to baseball's popularity by giving fans genuine hope that the next year would bring their team a championship.

Labor disputes, however, almost killed baseball's popularity. In 1981, the baseball season was marred by a bitter player strike that lasted from June 12 to the end of July and led to the cancellation of 713 games, a third of the schedule. The strike resulted from a dispute over compensation for players who switched teams as free agents. Several public opinion polls suggested widespread hostility toward the players, whose average salaries had ballooned with the emergence of free agency in the late 1970s. The crisis, brought about by the owners to alter or put an end to player free-agency, left a very sour feeling throughout the nation. Just four years later, proving that neither management nor the players' union had learned much from their previous conflict, another baseball strike was called. Thankfully, though, that midseason work stoppage lasted only two days.

Cal Ripken Jr. throwing to first base. **Reproduced by permission of AP/Wide World Photos.**

For all its problems, baseball provided fans with a great deal of plea-sure in the 1980s. Many ballplayers performed brilliantly and established some remarkable single-game, regular-season, postseason, and career records and achievements. Len Barker, Tom Browning, and Mike Witt each pitched perfect games during the decade. In all, the 1980s witnessed seventeen no-hitters, including Nolan Ryan's record-setting fifth. In 1986,

World Series Champions

Year	Winning Team	Losing Team
1980	Philadelphia Phillies (NL) 4	Kansas City Royals (AL) 2
1981	Los Angeles Dodgers (NL) 4	New York Yankees (AL) 2
1982	St. Louis Cardinals (NL) 4	Milwaukee Brewers (AL) 3
1983	Baltimore Orioles (AL) 4	Philadelphia Phillies (NL) 1
1984	Detroit Tigers (AL) 4	San Diego Padres (NL) 1
1985	Kansas City Royals (AL) 4	St. Louis Cardinals (NL) 3
1986	New York Mets (NL) 4	Boston Red Sox (AL) 3
1987	Minnesota Twins (AL) 4	St. Louis Cardinals (NL) 3
1988	Los Angeles Dodgers (NL) 4	Oakland Athletics (AL) 1
1989	Oakland Athletics (AL) 4	San Francisco Giants (NL) 0

Roger Clemens set a major-league record by striking out twenty hitters in a single game. That same season, Bob Horner tied a major-league record by slugging four home runs in a game.

From a single-season perspective, there were more than a few performances of historic note. George Brett hit a phenomenal .390 batting average in 1980, which remains the highest major-league batting average since Ted Williams hit .406 in 1941. In 1982, Rickey Henderson destroyed Lou Brock's single-season stolen base record by swiping 130 bases. Pitcher Dwight Gooden's 1985 season ranks among the greatest of all time: he led the National League (NL) in wins (24), ERA (1.53), and strikeouts (268). In 1988, Orel Hershiser set a major-league mark with 59 consecutive scoreless innings pitched, and Jose Canseco became the first player ever to steal forty bases and hit forty home runs in the same season.

Over the course of the decade, milestones were passed and dominant players emerged. Rollie Fingers set an all-time mark for saves with 341. Ferguson Jenkins become only the fourth pitcher to win one hundred games in both leagues. Steve Carlton became the all-time left-handed strikeout leader, ending up with 4,136. Wade Boggs won five American League (AL) batting crowns and had seven consecutive 200-hit seasons. Tony Gwynn won four NL batting titles. Rickey Henderson led the AL in stolen bases nine times, and Ozzie Smith won all ten NL Gold Glove awards at shortstop. Jack Morris was the decade's winningest pitcher with 162 victories.

❖ BASKETBALL: MAGIC AND BIRD AND A ROOKIE NAMED JORDAN

As the National Basketball Association (NBA) staggered toward the close of the 1970s, attendance was down and television ratings were declining. The public had become fed up with players' bouts with alcohol and drug abuse and their uninspired play. But in game six of the 1980 league finals between the Los Angeles Lakers and the Philadelphia 76ers, basketball began a remarkable comeback in America. The televised game showcased the talents of Earvin "Magic" Johnson, the Lakers rookie who, along with the Boston Celtics' Larry Bird, had riveted public attention in the NCAA finals a year earlier.

Johnson, filling in for injured veteran Kareem Abdul-Jabbar, put on a tremendous show. He collected 42 points, 15 rebounds, and 7 assists. It was a performance that foreshadowed the Lakers' nearly decade-long hold on the championship. From 1980 to 1989, the Lakers played for the title eight times, winning the championship five times. In the decade, clashes between Johnson's Lakers and Bird's Celtics revived fan interest and inspired fellow players toward remarkable individual and team accomplishments. In addition to the Lakers' success with Johnson, Boston with Bird in the lineup made it to the finals in 1981 and each year from 1984 to 1987, winning three titles. The level at which Bird and Johnson played and the heights to which they took their respective teams enthralled the American public. By decade's end, the league had reached new financial and popular heights.

Looking to spice up the NBA, the league's board of governors voted to introduce a three-point shot into the game at the start of the 1980 and 1981 season. The shot had worked well in the old American Basketball Association (ABA), leading to higher scores and last-second drama. The NBA was in need of both elements and was willing to alter the shape of the game in order to get them. Although teams and players alike were slow at first to utilize the three-point shot, fans were excited by the new rule and its potential to inject drama into the game at any moment. By the end of the 1980s, teams had collectively attempted more than 13,400 three-point shots a season, hitting nearly one-third of them. Efficient three-point marksmen like Dale Ellis and Danny Ainge managed to extend their careers well into the 1990s because of their ability to "knock down the trey" consistently.

The 1984 college draft featured some amazing future stars of the NBA: Hakeem Olajuwon (picked by Houston), Charles Barkley (picked by

Philadelphia), and John Stockton (picked by Utah). However, the player picked third in the first round by the Chicago Bulls would become a superstar: North Carolina junior Michael Jordan. His impact on the league was immediate and long-lasting. Jordan won the NBA Rookie of the Year award in 1985. The following year, he averaged 37.1 points per game and became the first player since Wilt Chamberlain to score more than three thousand points in a season. He signed unprecedented shoe contracts with Nike and established an amazing career in commercials within his first two years in the league. More important, he transcended the game and transformed the fortunes of his franchise. By the early 1990s, Jordan had the Bulls poised to win three consecutive NBA championships.

The NBA was revived not only by the playing exploits of Johnson, Bird, and Jordan but also by keen marketing changes. Borrowing ideas from the ABA and Major League Baseball, the NBA turned its All-Star game into a fan-friendly extravaganza, complete with slam-dunk and three-point-shooting contests and an old-timers' game. By the end of the 1980s, it was clear that the changes had paid off. The league broke its attendance record seven straight years. Player salaries rose 177 percent (from an average of $325,000 to $900,000 by decade's end), and television fees skyrocketed from $22 million per year to more than $150 million. The NBA was back in business.

❖ FOOTBALL: LAWSUITS AND LABOR DISPUTES

Similar to professional baseball, the National Football League (NFL) suffered through two significant labor disputes during the 1980s. Both led to the suspension of play. In 1982, a fifty-seven-day strike resulted in the cancellation of seven weeks of play. The strike occurred after the league signed a five-year, $2.1 billion contract with the three major television networks. The NFL Players Association (NFLPA) responded by demanding a larger cut of the guarantees, 55 percent of the league's gross revenues. NFL team owners kept camps closed throughout the strike in the fear that a series of makeshift games conducted with replacement players might tarnish the league's image. After a mediator was finally brought in, the NFLPA agreed to a contract in which the team owners guaranteed to spend $1.6 billion over four years on players' salaries.

Two games into the 1987 and 1988 season, a second strike occurred. This time, teams reloaded their rosters with replacement players immediately, and the league determined that any games played during the strike would count in the final league standings. The NFLPA initially demanded unlimited free agency for league players; they later proposed freedom of movement after a four-year tenure in the league. Despite the fact that the average NFL career is less than the four-year minimum proposed, the

*OPPOSITE PAGE
Striking San Diego
Chargers football players
(foreground) looking over
newly hired replacement
players during the second
day of the NFL players
strike in 1987.* **Reproduced
by permission of the
Corbis Corporation.**

Super Bowl Champions

Year	Winning Team	Losing Team
1980	Pittsburgh Steelers 31	Los Angeles Rams 19
1981	Oakland Raiders 27	Philadelphia Eagles 10
1982	San Francisco 49ers 26	Cincinnati Bengals 21
1983	Washington Redskins 27	Miami Dolphins 17
1984	Los Angeles Raiders 38	Washington Redskins 9
1985	San Francisco 49ers 38	Miami Dolphins 16
1986	Chicago Bears 46	New England Patriots 10
1987	New York Giants 39	Denver Broncos 20
1988	Washington Redskins 42	Denver Broncos 10
1989	San Francisco 49ers 20	Cincinnati Bengals 16

owners rejected the condition outright. Failing to reach a new agreement, the players' union ended the strike after twenty-four days and three weeks of replacement games. The owners did pay for their unyielding position, at least in the short term, by losing over $100 million in potential revenue due to the suspension of play.

Further disruption in the NFL in the 1980s was largely due to the actions of the Oakland Raiders' managing general partner, Al Davis. He decided to move the Raiders from Oakland to Los Angeles for the start of the 1982 football season because Los Angeles offered a larger venue and the opportunity to operate in one of the country's media capitals. Davis's decision, though, violated the league constitution, which required the approval of three-quarters of the league's owners before a franchise could relocate. When the NFL tried to block the move, Davis, the Raiders, and the Los Angeles Coliseum Commission sued the league. Following a five-week trial, a jury ruled against the NFL, and the Raiders went on to win the 1984 Super Bowl under their new name, the Los Angeles Raiders.

Davis's legal triumph opened the way for further movement. In the early morning of March 29, 1984, Baltimore Colts owner Robert Irsay stealthily moved all of the Colts' possessions to Indiana with a fleet of moving vans, thus establishing the Indianapolis Colts in a sleek new domed stadium. Irsay's abandonment of Baltimore left a sour taste in the mouths of true Colts fans. Finally, in 1988, the St. Louis Cardinals moved to Phoenix, thanks to the efforts of team owner Bill Bidwill. The move, however, was justified. St. Louis, long acknowledged as a baseball town, consistently had trouble attracting a substantial football crowd.

In spite of the various lawsuits and legal disputes off the field, the NFL thrived because of some marvelous performances on it. In particular, Chicago's Walter Payton, known as "Sweetness," erased the bitterness of league turmoil with his unique blend of grace, agility, and power. When Payton did not stutter-step a lineman off his feet or beat the linebacker to the corner, he simply flattened an unsuspecting cornerback with a stiff-arm or a lowered shoulder. In 1984, Payton broke Jim Brown's all-time rushing mark of 12,312 yards, and by the time he retired in 1987, he had tacked another 4,000 yards onto the standard.

Without a doubt, the dominant team of the 1980s was the San Francisco 49ers. They crushed the opposition with a precise, nearly unstoppable offense. Designed by their innovative head coach, Bill Walsh, and mastered by quarterback Joe Montana, the San Francisco system depended on short passes and players who could run after they caught the ball. It did not hurt that Walsh coached two of the best players ever to play their positions, Montana and receiver Jerry Rice. In 1982, using an assortment of trick plays and new formations, the 49ers confused the Cincinnati Bengals from the beginning of the game and won their first Super Bowl. In 1985, Montana simply outgunned the Dolphins' Dan Marino in Super Bowl XIX, hitting on 24 of 35 passes for 331 yards and three touchdowns. Then, after four years of missing the Super Bowl, the 49ers returned in 1989 and 1990 to win the first back-to-back titles since the great Pittsburgh teams of the 1970s.

❖ GOLF: NICKLAUS RETURNS AND THE GAME GOES INTERNATIONAL

At the beginning of the 1980s, legendary golfer Jack Nicklaus was, by many accounts, growing old and losing his competitive edge. At forty, his drives were not as long as they once were and his legendary concentration often seemed to lapse at critical times. But at the 1980 U.S. Open, after a two-year winless streak and endless tinkering with his swing mechanics and short game, Nicklaus unexpectedly seized control with an Open-record 63 in the first round. He went on to lead the tournament from start to finish, wrapping up his fourth Open championship. The title was Nicklaus's eighteenth major championship, five more than anyone else in history. But he was not through that year.

PGA Player of the Year

Year	Player
1980	Tom Watson
1981	Bill Rogers
1982	Tom Watson
1983	Hal Sutton
1984	Tom Watson
1985	Lanny Wadkins
1986	Bob Tway
1987	Paul Azinger
1988	Curtis Strange
1989	Tom Kite

In August, the rejuvenated Nicklaus routed the field in the Professional Golfers' Association (PGA) Championship, winning by seven shots on the treacherous Oak Hill course in Rochester, New York. By claiming two major titles in 1980, Nicklaus accomplished an incredible feat. He had won majors in four different decades dating back to his 1959 U.S. Amateur Championship. His feat confirmed what many knew: He was the greatest golfer the game had ever known.

If Nicklaus's victories in 1980 surprised those who thought his best golf was behind him, then his winning the 1986 Masters Tournament at the age of forty-six must have seemed unthinkable. Nicklaus began the final round five shots behind the leader, Greg Norman, and had eight players ahead of him on the leader board. Having missed a series of relatively easy putts on the front nine, Nicklaus suddenly caught fire, shooting a phenomenal 30 on the back nine for a round of 65 to win his sixth green jacket.

Despite Nicklaus's stunning comeback, the early years of the decade belonged to Tom Watson. In the mid-1970s, Watson endured a reputation as a choker (performer who collapses under pressure.) after letting two U.S. Open titles slip from his grasp, but in 1977 he bested Nicklaus in two thrilling matches at the Masters and the British Open. By the 1980s, Watson was in contention nearly every week. Each year he seemed to set a new season-earnings record, gathering PGA Player of the Year honors in 1977 through 1980, 1982, and 1984 (more than any other golfer in history), and winning a total of eight major championships between 1975 and 1983.

During the decade, golf increasingly became an international game as the customary dominance of American players began to fade. On the Ladies Professional Golf Association (LPGA) tour, England's Laura Davies and Sweden's Liselotte Neumann won U.S. Opens in 1987 and 1988, and Ayako Okamoto of Japan was selected as the 1987 LPGA Player of the Year after leading all female golfers in earnings. South Africa's Sally Little continued to win frequently on the women's circuit, capturing three different major championships during the decade. On the men's tour, the presence of international players was even more pronounced. European players won nearly half of the Masters and British Opens contested during the 1980s. Australians David Graham and Greg Norman each captured one major during that span. At age twenty-three, Seve Ballesteros from Spain became the youngest champion ever at the Masters when he won the tournament in 1980.

Perhaps the most telling sign of the European rise came in the Ryder Cup series, a biannual team competition pitting an American squad against a contingent of golfers from Europe. When the Europeans captured the cup in 1985, it was their first victory since 1957. They proved the feat was no fluke by winning again in 1987, and after a tie in 1989, retained the cup into the 1990s.

❖ HOCKEY: THE "GREAT ONE" APPEARS

In the 1980s, the National Hockey League (NHL) achieved new heights of popularity. This stemmed in part from the interest in the sport generated when the U.S. hockey team shocked the world by upsetting the mighty Soviet Union and later winning the gold medal at the 1980 Winter Olympics. The U.S. hockey team's victory brought the sport to millions of viewers who were caught up in the excitement of the unfolding national drama but who had no previous knowledge of or interest in the game.

As the American public tuned in to the NHL, they saw the beginning of the New York Islanders' dynasty. During the first half of the decade, the Islanders' combination of offensive firepower and defensive ruggedness proved to be too much for their opponents. Like the Montreal Canadiens of the late 1970s, the Islanders of the early 1980s thoroughly dominated the league. With perennial all-stars such as forward Mike Bossy, center Bryan Trottier, defenseman Denis Potvin, and goalie Billy Smith, the Islanders won four consecutive Stanley Cups between 1980 and 1983. Noted for their fierce competitiveness and poise, the aging and injured

Stanley Cup Champions

Year	Winning Team	Losing Team
1980	New York Islanders 4	Philadelphia Flyers 2
1981	New York Islanders 4	Minnesota North Stars 1
1982	New York Islanders 4	Vancouver Canucks 0
1983	New York Islanders 4	Edmonton Oilers 0
1984	Edmonton Oilers 4	New York Islanders 1
1985	Edmonton Oilers 4	Philadelphia Flyers 1
1986	Montreal Canadiens 4	Calgary Flames 1
1987	Edmonton Oilers 4	Philadelphia Flyers 3
1988	Edmonton Oilers 4	Boston Bruins 0
1989	Calgary Flames 4	Montreal Canadiens 2

Islanders reached the Stanley Cup finals yet again in 1984, but were overwhelmed four games to one by the speedy Edmonton Oilers, whom the Isles had swept in the finals the year before. With that victory, the Oilers began their own dynasty, emerging as the best team in hockey for the rest of the decade. They were led by "The Great One," Wayne Gretzky.

When Gretzky joined the Edmonton Oilers of the World Hockey Association (WHA) in 1978, he was seventeen years old, the youngest player ever in professional hockey. At the end of the season, he was named WHA Rookie of the Year. The next season the Oilers merged into the NHL and Gretzky became the youngest player to ever win the Hart Trophy, the league's MVP award. During his nine years in Edmonton, Gretzky won the Hart Trophy eight times. In his third year in the NHL, he led the league in goals (92), assists (120), and total points (212), all of which were single-season records. He established more than fifty other regular-season and career scoring records. In playoff action, Getzky became the all-time points leader. In two of the four years in which he led the Oilers to Stanley Cup titles in the 1980s, Gretzky was voted MVP of the playoffs.

As Gretzky continued to rewrite the record book and win championships, his popularity and legend grew. It therefore came as a tremendous surprise to the sporting world in 1988 when Gretzky was traded to the Los Angeles Kings in a multiplayer, multimillion-dollar deal the summer after he led the Oilers to their fourth Stanley Cup. With the Kings, Gretzky continued his unparalleled success. In his first season in Los Angeles, he scored 168 points and earned his ninth Hart Trophy. Early the next season, he broke hockey legend Gordie Howe's all-time scoring record of 1,850 points. Howe had set the record over the course of twenty-six seasons; Gretzky broke it in less than ten.

❖ TENNIS: THE GENIUS OF MCENROE AND THE POWER GAME

John McEnroe dominated tennis during the first half of the 1980s like few before him. After losing the 1980 Wimbledon title to Bjorn Borg in a match many consider one of the best ever played, McEnroe bounced back with the second of three consecutive U.S. Open titles. Between 1980 and 1984, he won seven Grand Slam singles titles (including three at Wimbledon), nine doubles championships with Peter Fleming, and was ranked as the world's number one male player at year's end four times. By the end of his career in the early 1990s, McEnroe had won seventy-seven tournament titles to finish third on the all-time list.

As is often the case, however, numbers tell only part of the story. In a world of hard hitters, McEnroe played finesse tennis, reminiscent of Ken Rosewall and Rod Laver, two legendary Australian players. His command of the men's tour inspired critics and colleagues. McEnroe's game was instinctive, inventive, occasionally overpowering, but always captivating for fans and frustrating for opponents.

For all his brilliance, McEnroe also represented what many considered to be the worst of tennis in the 1980s. A trend toward crude and loud behavior, initiated by Ilie Nastase and Jimmy Connors in the 1970s, was continued by McEnroe and others in the 1980s. Sometimes unable to control himself during key matches, McEnroe criticized officials for what he deemed to be missed calls. He loudly complained about fan noise and movement during matches. Many thought such behavior was destroying the game. In an era when the public was quick to criticize athletes, the men's tennis tour provided critics with a great deal of ammunition. Fearing the loss of tennis fans, United States Tennis Association began leveling fines and enforcing policies of conduct on a more regular basis beginning in 1983.

Another change in the 1980s was the way tennis was played on the professional level. Due to the development and introduction of stronger composite and graphite rackets, tennis became a power game. In the latter half of the decade, several players had fashioned their games to fit the new technology and were claiming titles and high rankings. Many were impressed by the new punch the game offered, but others were concerned.

U.S. Open Tennis Tournament Champions

Year	Male	Female
1980	John McEnroe	Chris Evert Lloyd
1981	John McEnroe	Tracy Austin
1982	Jimmy Connors	Chris Evert Lloyd
1983	Jimmy Connors	Martina Navratilova
1984	John McEnroe	Martina Navratilova
1985	Ivan Lendl	Hana Mandlikova
1986	Ivan Lendl	Martina Navratilova
1987	Ivan Lendl	Martina Navratilova
1988	Mats Wilander	Steffi Graf
1989	Boris Becker	Steffi Graf

While Ivan Lendl, the world's number-one ranked male player from 1985 to 1987, and Boris Becker, the men's Wimbledon champion in 1985, 1986, and 1989, played tennis at a high level and were excellent shot makers, other players were winning without as much skill. Their strategy was to pound their opponents into the court. By the close of the 1980s, some in the tennis world called for the return of wood rackets, particularly on the men's tour. Those calls were largely ignored, though, and the boom-or-bust game continued to thrive well into the 1990s.

❖ THE OLYMPICS

The 1980 Winter Olympics, held in Lake Placid, New York, featured 839 male and 233 female athletes representing thirty-seven nations. It was the second time the Winter Games were held in the tiny upstate New York town, the first time being in 1932. American athletes finished third in the final medal standings, winning twelve medals, half of which were gold. Most importantly, they provided the Games with two of its most extraordinary, memorable, and historic performances.

Over the course of eight days, twenty-one-year-old American speed skater Eric Heiden won gold medals and set Olympic records in all five of the events in which he participated: the 500-, 1,000-, 1,500-, 5,000-, and 10,000-meter races. In so doing, he became the first athlete ever to win five

U.S. hockey players celebrate on the ice after winning the gold medal at the 1980 Olympic Games. *Reproduced by permission of AP/Wide World Photos.*

gold medals in individual events in one Olympics. He alone won more gold medals than any American team had in the Winter Games since 1932.

One of the greatest upsets in the history of American sport and the Olympic Games occurred in 1980 when the U.S. men's hockey team beat the Soviet Union four to three. The infectious joy expressed by the American players after the surprising victory quickly swept across the nation, leading to patriotic celebrations. Two days later, the inspired American team beat Finland four to two to win the Olympic gold medal, again prompting a national outpouring of pride and joy.

The Summer Games that year were held in Moscow, marking the first time the Olympics were held in a communist nation. Representing eighty nations were 4,093 male and 1,124 female athletes. To protest the recent Soviet invasion of the country of Afghanistan, the United States led sixty-four other nations in a boycott of the Games. Many Olympic purists argued that the Olympics should be divorced from politics, but others pointed out that politics had always been present in the Games. Although the decision by President Jimmy Carter (1924–) understandably angered many American athletes, he remained firm behind his position.

Four years later, the 1984 Winter Olympics were held in Sarajevo, Yugoslavia, with 1,000 male and 274 female athletes from forty-nine countries competing. The American team won a total of eight medals and did particularly well in the alpine events. Bill Johnson became the first American to win a gold medal in the Olympic downhill skiing event. Debbie Armstrong and Christin Cooper finished first and second in the women's giant slalom, while twins Phil and Steve Mahre finished first and second in the men's slalom. The rest of the U.S. medals came in figure skating, led by three-time world champion Scott Hamilton, who won the men's competition and set a new Olympic record in the process.

Gold medal gymnast Mary Lou Retton during the 1984 Olympic Games. Reproduced by permission of Archive Photos, Inc.

The political controversy surrounding the Summer Games in Moscow carried over to those held in Los Angeles in 1984. A few communist countries joined the Soviet Union in a revenge boycott, but 140 nations still took part, represented by 5,230 male and 1,567 female athletes. The United States

S ince it began in 1903, the Tour de France has become what many consider to be the world's grandest and perhaps greatest sporting adventure. The cycling race, held over three weeks every July, winds its way through France and neighboring countries, covering more than two thousand miles, before finishing in the French capital of Paris. Thousands of spectators line the route every year; millions more watch the race on television.

No American had ever finished in the top three positions in the race until 1984, when Greg LeMond finished third. Born in Lakewood, California, in 1961, LeMond had become a professional cyclist in the early 1980s. In 1986, in his third Tour de France, LeMond emerged victorious, despite being constantly threatened by his own teammate Bernard Hinault. His victory, the first for an American in the history of the Tour, catapulted him into the media spotlight.

The following April, while hunting in California, LeMond was accidentally shot by his brother-in-law. Incredibly, he survived the life-threatening injury, but doctors had to leave more than thirty shotgun pellets imbedded in his body. Against all odds, he began a comeback in hopes not only of reentering the world of professional cycling but of winning the Tour once again.

In 1989, LeMond did just that, overcoming a lead by Frenchman Laurent Fignon to win by eight seconds, the narrowest margin of victory ever in the history of the race. He won his third, and final, Tour de France the following year, then retired from competitive cycling in 1994 because of a muscular disorder.

finished on top of the medal standings, winning 174 medals, 83 of which were gold. Of the many American stars at the Games, the brightest was twenty-three-year-old sprinter and long jumper Carl Lewis. He won three individual gold medals (in the 100 meters, the 200 meters, and the long jump) and he anchored the gold medal-winning 4 x 100-meter relay team.

Although Lewis captured more gold medals, gymnast Mary Lou Retton probably captured more hearts. The four-foot nine-inch sixteen-year-old won the individual all-around competition with a perfect score in the final event. It was the first all-around gymnastics victory for an American in any international competition.

Other notable American performances included Greg Louganis's golds in the ten-meter platform diving competition and the springboard event. Swimmers Carrie Steinseiffer and Nancy Hogshead won three gold medals apiece. The men's volleyball team won the gold medal, while the boxing team won a record nine gold medals. Valerie Brisco-Hooks became the first sprinter to win both the 200 meters and the 400 meters in the same Games, and Joan Benoit won the first women's Olympic marathon.

The 1988 Winter Olympics, held in Calgary, Canada, marked the first time the Winter Games were extended to sixteen days. Representing 57 nations were 1,100 male and 313 female athletes. The American team did not fare well, finishing with only six medals, two of them gold. Brian Boitano won the men's figure skating competition, while speed skater Bonnie Blair won gold in the 500-meter race, setting new Olympic and world records in the process. Blair later won a bronze in the 1,000 meters to become the only double medalist on the U.S. team.

The 1988 Summer Games, held in Seoul, South Korea, drew 6,279 male and 2,186 female athletes from a record 160 countries. The American team won ninety-four medals, of which thirty-six were gold. Both Greg Louganis and Carl Lewis repeated their gold medal-winning performances from the last Olympics. Louganis won gold in the springboard event, while Lewis was awarded the gold medal in the 100 meters after Canadian Ben Johnson, who actually won the race, was stripped of the medal after he had tested positive for performance-enhancing drugs.

The most successful and flamboyant female athlete of the Olympics was Florence Griffith Joyner. Dubbed "Flo-Jo," Griffith Joyner won gold medals in the 100- and 200-meter races. Then, she ran the third leg of the gold medal-winning 4 x 100-meter relay team. Finally, she anchored the silver medal-winning 4 x 400-meter relay squad. Jackie Joyner-Kersee, Griffith Joyner's sister-in-law, performed no less spectacularly. She bested her own world record in the seven-event heptathlon and later won her second gold medal of the Games in the long jump competition.

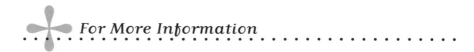

For More Information

BOOKS

Bird, Larry, with Bob Ryan. *Drive: The Story of My Life.* Reissue ed. New York: Bantam Books, 1990.

Dryden, Steve. *Total Gretzky: The Magic, the Legend, the Numbers.* Toronto, Ontario: McClelland and Stewart, 1999.

Greenspan, Bud. *Frozen in Time: The Greatest Moments at the Winter Olympics.* Santa Monica, CA: General Publishing Group, 1997.

Johnson, Earvin "Magic," and William Novak. *My Life.* New York: Random House, 1992.

McEnroe, John, with James Kaplan. *You Cannot Be Serious.* New York: Putnam, 2002.

Nicklaus, Jack, and Ken Bowden. *Jack Nicklaus: My Story.* New York: Simon and Schuster, 1997.

Wiener, Paul. *Joe Montana.* New York: Chelsea House, 1995.

WEB SITES

LPGA Official Website. http://www.lpga.com/ (accessed on July 29, 2002).

NBA.com. http://www.nba.com (accessed on July 29, 2002).

NFL.com. http://www.nfl.com/ (accessed on July 29, 2002).

NHL.com-The National Hockey League Web Site. http://www.nhl.com (accessed on July 29, 2002).

The Official Site of Major League Baseball. http://mlb.mlb.com/NASApp/mlb/mlb/homepage/mlb_homepage.jsp (accessed on July 29, 2002).

The Official Website of the Olympic Movement. http://www.olympic.org/uk/index_uk.asp (accessed on July 29, 2002).

PGA of America. http://www.pga.com/ (accessed on July 29, 2002).

Tour de France. http://www.letour.fr/indexus.html (accessed on July 29, 2002).

U.S. Tennis Association. http://www.usta.com/index.html (accessed on July 29, 2002).

Where to Learn More

Books

Arenson, David, and Marilyn Werden. *Rambo Reagan: Over 1,400 Mind-Bending Trivia Questions About the '80s*. Chicago, IL: Contemporary Books, 1996.

Feinstein, Stephen. *The 1980s: From Ronald Reagan to MTV*. Berkeley Heights, NJ: Enslow, 2000.

Gaslin, Glenn, and Rick Porter. *The Complete, Cross-Referenced Guide to the Baby Buster Generation's Collective Unconscious*. New York: Boulevard Books, 1998.

Gross, Nigel. *The 1980s*. New York: HarperCollins, 2000.

Kallen, Stuart A. *The 1980s*. San Diego, CA: Lucent Books, 1999.

Levy, Peter B. *Encyclopedia of the Reagan-Bush Years*. Westport, CN: Greenwood Press, 1996.

Rettenmund, Matthew. *Totally Awesome 80s: A Lexicon of the Music, Videos, Movies, TV Shows, Stars, and Trends of That Decadent Decade*. New York: St. Martin's Press, 1996.

Slansky, Paul. *The Clothes Have No Emperor: A Chronicle of the American '80s*. New York: Simon and Schuster, 1989.

Time-Life Books, ed. *Pride and Prosperity: The 80s*. Alexandria, VA: Time-Life Books, 1999.

Torr, James D. *The 1980s*. San Diego, CA: Greenhaven Press, 2000.

Web Sites

American Cultural History: 1980–1989. http://www.nhmccd.cc.tx.us/contracts/lrc/kc/decade80.html (accessed on June 1, 2002).

Where to Learn More

Anything At All About the 1980s. http://library.thinkquest.org/17823/data/ (accessed on June 1, 2002).

Biography of America: Contemporary History. http://www.learner.org/biographyof america/prog25/index.html (accessed on June 1, 2002).

1860–2000 General History: 1980s. http://cdcga.org/HTMLs/decades/1980s.htm (accessed on June 1, 2002).

History Channel. http://www.historychannel.com/index.html (accessed on June 1, 2002).

History from the Eighties. http://www.huberspace.com/80s/history/ (accessed on June 1, 2002)

Map: Political Systems of the World in the 1980s. http://users.erols.com/mwhite28/ govt1980.htm (accessed on June 1, 2002).

Media History Timeline: 1980s. http://www.mediahistory.umn.edu/time/1980s.html (accessed on June 1, 2002).

1980s Flashback: 1980–1989. http://www.1980sflashback.com/ (accessed on June 1, 2002).

Nobel e-Museum. http://www.nobel.se/ (accessed June 1, 2002).

Official Website of the Olympic Movement. http://www.olympic.org/uk/index_uk. asp (accessed on June 1, 2002).

20th Century American Culture. http://members.aol.com/TeacherNet/20CC.html (accessed on June 1, 2002).

20th Century Decades: 1980–1989 Decade. http://dewey.chs.chico.k12.ca.us/decs8. html (accessed on June 1, 2002).

20th Century Fashion History: 1980s–1990s. http://www.costumegallery.com/1980. htm (accessed on June 1, 2002).

20th Century History. http://history1900s.about.com/ (accessed on June 1, 2002).

Index